Ali
The musical

Based on the original story of 'Alice's Adventures In Wonderland',
by Lewis Carroll.

Adapted and dramatised by Mark and Helen Johnson
and Richard Davis

For children aged 7-14 (KS 2-3). Adaptable for younger children.

If you wish to adapt this play, it is recommended that you refer to the original script
(*Penguin Popular Classics - ISBN 0-14-062086-9*)

LIST OF SONGS

CAST OF CHARACTERS

Narrator
Lewis Carroll

Principal Players
(*with dialogue & suggested solo parts*)

Alice

White Rabbit

Mouse

Mad Hatter

Queen Of Hearts

Mock Turtle

Gryphon

King Of Hearts

Minor Characters
(*with some dialogue*)

Lory

Dodo

Fish and Frog Footman

Duchess

Cook

March Hare

Dormouse

Two, Five and Seven of Hearts

Knave of Hearts

Groups/Extras
(*numbers may vary to suit circumstances*)

Lorina and Edith - Alice's sisters

Revd. Duckworth

Assorted Animals and Birds

Royal Procession Ensemble

Executioners (*two plus*)

Dancers
(*minimum seven*)

Singers

Alice
The musical

ACT ONE

OVERTURE (Ent'racte could be used as an alternative)

Lewis Carroll — Many a day we rowed together on that quiet stream, the three little maidens, Duckworth and I - and many a fairy tale had been told for their benefit. Yet none of these many tales got written down: they lived and died, like summer midges, each in its golden afternoon, until there came a day when one of my listeners begged that the tale be written out for her....

ALL IN A GOLDEN AFTERNOON

ALL

All in a golden afternoon
Under the skies of cloudless blue,
Leisurely gliding time away,
Heading upstream to find some shade,
Sleepily drifting on our way that dreamy English summer's day.

All in a golden afternoon
Eager for stories wild and new,
Three little ladies named 'Liddell'
Longed for a fable to be told.
What can a single voice avail against three tongues that beg a tale?
Tell us a story, tell us a story...

All in a golden afternoon
Tales of imagination grew.
Alice the dream-child took our hands
Through many adventures, all unplanned.
Slowly the tales of wonderland did come to us as now they stand.
Tell us the story, tell us the story, tell us the story please.

Lewis Carroll — (*Sitting at writing desk*) Full many a year has slipped away since that 'golden afternoon', but I can call it up almost as clearly as if it were yesterday - the cloudless blue above, the watery mirror below, the boat drifting idly on its way, the tinkle of the drops that fell from the oars, as they waved so sleepily to and fro, and the three eager faces, hungry for news of fairyland. (*Starting to write*). Alice was beginning to get very tired of sitting by her sister on the bank, and of having nothing to do. Once or twice she had peeped into the book her sister was reading. (***The remainder of Lewis Carroll's lines can be read, as he 'writes' the story***).

Alice — What is the use of a book without pictures or conversation in it?

Lewis Carroll — She was considering whether the pleasure of making a daisy-chain would be worth the trouble of getting up and picking the daisies, when suddenly, a White Rabbit with pink eyes ran close by her.

I'M LATE!

I'm late! I'm late! **I'm getting in a terrible state, I'll have to hurry.** **Better get a move on 'cause I'm running out of time.** **I'm late! I'm late!** **I haven't got a moment to waste, I'm getting worried.** **What am I to do? I'm going out of my mind!**	***WHITE RABBIT***

I'm late! I'm late!
If the Duchess has a minute to wait she'll have my head off.
Better get a move on, 'cause I'm running out of time.
I'm late! I'm late!
If I cannot keep this crucial date there'll be no let off.
What am I to do? I'm going out of my mind!........I'M LATE!!

Lewis Carroll — Burning with curiosity, Alice ran across the field after it. Fortunately, she was just in time to see it pop down a large rabbit-hole under the hedge. Alice went down after it, never once considering how in the world she would get out again. The rabbit-hole went straight on like a tunnel, and then dipped suddenly down. Alice found herself falling down a very deep well.

DOWN, DOWN, DOWN — *(Song & Dance)*

CHORUS ***Down, down, down - I feel I'm falling through the ground.*** ***Down, down, down - I'm falling, slowly, falling down.*** ***Down, down, down - My world is turning all around.*** ***Down, down, down - I'm feeling sleepy feelings now.***	***ALL***
What's going to happen? **It seems I've been falling** **For miles unending** **And when will it stop?**	***ALICE***
CHORUS	
Falling in darkness **Past cupboards and bookshelves** **I'm looking around me** **At pictures and maps.**	***ALICE***
CHORUS	
Where am I going? **I can't get my bearings.** **I've gone such a distance** **Where will I end up?**	***ALICE***

Lewis Carroll — Down she came upon a heap of sticks and dry leaves, and the fall was over. Alice jumped onto her feet in a moment. It was dark overhead and in front was another long passage. The White Rabbit was still in sight, hurrying along it.

White Rabbit — Oh my ears and whiskers! How late it's getting! (*exits*)

Alice — What an unusual hallway! I do believe I'm in the Rabbit's house. Oh, he's left a key.

	I wonder if it opens one of these doors.
Lewis Carroll	Alas! either the locks were too large, or the key was too small. At any rate, it wouldn't open any of them. Suddenly, Alice came upon a low curtain she had not noticed before, and behind it was a little door about fifteen inches high. She knelt down, opened the door and looked along the passage.
Alice	The loveliest garden you ever saw!

MY LOVELY GARDEN

Who can find my lovely garden? *ALICE*
It's the place I'd really like to be.
Safe inside my lovely garden
With the sunlight streaming down on me.

CHORUS ***Fountains pure, and grass so green.*** *ALL*
I can hear birds singing in the trees.
I must find my lovely garden,
It's the place I visit in my dreams.

INSTRUMENTAL BACKING UNDER DIALOGUE:

Alice	Oh, how I wish I could get out of this dark hall, and wander about among those beds of bright flowers and those cool fountains, but I can't even get my head through the doorway, and even if my head would go through, it would be of very little use without my shoulders. (*Sighs*). If only I could find a way!

CHORUS
Repeat last line

Alice	I wish I could shut up like a telescope. Perhaps I might find a book of rules that would show me how. (*Walks back to the table*). This little bottle certainly wasn't here before. 'Drink Me!' - I shall look first and see whether it's marked 'poison' or not. Anything marked 'poison' is sure to disagree with you sooner or later, if you drink too much of it. This looks OK, though. (*Drinks from it*). Mm! Very nice! A mixed sort of flavour - cherry tart, custard, pineapple, roast turkey, toffee and hot buttered toast. (*Drinks some more*). Delicious! What a curious feeling! I must be getting smaller!
Lewis Carroll	And so it was indeed. She was now only ten inches high. Alice felt a little nervous about shrinking any further. After a while, finding nothing more happened, she decided to go to the garden at once. But, alas, for poor Alice! When she got to the door, she found she had forgotten the key. And when she went back to the table to get it, she couldn't possibly reach it. Try as she might, it was no use. Alice sat down and cried.
Alice	There's no use in crying like that! I advise you to leave off this minute.
Lewis Carroll	Suddenly, she noticed a small cake beside her. The words 'Eat me' were written on it in currants.
Alice	Well I shall eat it! If it makes me grow larger, I can reach the key, and if it makes me grow smaller, I can creep under the door. Either way I'll get into the garden. (*Holding her hand on her head*). Which way? Which way? (*Eats some more*). Curiouser and curiouser! Now I'm opening out like the tallest telescope that ever was! Goodbye feet!

Lewis Carroll — Alice was now more than nine feet high. At once, she took the little golden key, and hurried off to the garden door. Lying down on one side, it was all she could do to look into the garden with one eye. To try and get through was more hopeless than ever. She sat down and began to cry again.

Alice — You ought to be ashamed of yourself - a great girl like you, to go on crying like this. Stop this moment, I tell you!

Lewis Carroll — But she went on all the same, shedding gallons of tears, until there was a large pool of tears all around her. Suddenly, she heard a little pattering of feet in the distance.

White Rabbit — Oh! The Duchess, the Duchess! Won't she be savage if I've kept her waiting!

I'M LATE! (Reprise)

I'm late! I'm late! *WHITE RABBIT*
If the Duchess has a minute to wait she'll have my head off.
Better get a move on, 'cause I'm running out of time.
I'm late! I'm late!
If I cannot keep this crucial date there'll be no let off.
What am I to do? I'm going out of my mind!........I'M LATE!!

Alice — If you please, sir...

White Rabbit — (*Startled*). I can't stop now. I'll be late! (*Hurries off, dropping gloves and fan*).

Alice — (*Picks them up*). Dear, dear. How queer everything is today. (*Fans herself and starts to shrink*). Goodness! I'm shrinking again. It must be the fan. (*Throws it on the floor*). I never was so small as this before, never!

Lewis Carroll — As she said these words, her foot slipped, and in another moment, splash! She was up to her chin in water. At first she thought she'd somehow fallen into the sea, but soon realised that she was in the pool of tears which she had wept when she was nine feet high.

I WISH I HADN'T CRIED SO MUCH

CHORUS ***I wish I hadn't cried so much,*** *ALL*
I wish I hadn't cried so much.
Now everything has changed and nothing is the same at all.
I wish I hadn't cried so much,
I wish I hadn't cried so much,
When only yesterday my life was not unusual.

I'm sinking and I'm sighing, *ALICE*
For all my silly crying.
I really wonder why I'm here at all.
I'm shrinking then I'm growing,
I'm coming and I'm going.
I'm tired of never knowing who I am.

CHORUS

This place is topsy-turvy, *ALICE*
It's all a bit un-nerving,
'Cause none of what I've learned is quite the same.

This wonderland I've entered
Is full of such adventure,
But just for now I'd settle for a change.

CHORUS

Look at me, what a sight! *ALICE*
I wish I hadn't cried, I wish I hadn't cried so much.

Lewis Carroll — Just then she heard something splashing about in the pool a little way off, and she swam nearer to make out what it was. At first, she thought it must be a walrus or a hippopotamus, but then she remembered how small she was now. She soon made out that it was only a mouse that had slipped into the pool like herself.

Alice — O mouse! Do you know the way out of here? I'm very tired of swimming about like this. O mouse! Perhaps it doesn't understand English. Perhaps it's a French mouse. I don't know much French. Let me see. "Ou est ma chatte?" Oh, I do beg your pardon. I quite forgot you didn't like cats.

Mouse — Not like cats! Would you like cats if you were me?

Alice — Well, perhaps not.

Mouse — Nasty, low, vulgar things! Don't let me hear any more about them again!

Alice — Are you - are you fond of - of dogs? (*No reply*). There's such a nice little dog near our house, I should like to show you!

Mouse — Cats! Dogs! 'Nice little things?!'

Alice — Oh dear. Now I've offended it again. Mouse, dear, do come back! We won't talk about cats or dogs if you don't like them!

Mouse — (*Turns round and swims slowly back*). Let's swim to shore, and then I'll tell you my history. Then you'll understand why it is I hate cats and dogs.

Lewis Carroll — It was high time for them to go. The pool was getting quite crowded with the birds and animals that had fallen into it. There was a duck and a Dodo, a Lory and several other curious creatures. Alice led the way, and the whole party swam to the shore. What a queer-looking party they were, assembled on the bank. The first question of course, was how to get dry.

Mouse — Sit down, all of you, and listen to me. Ahem! Silence, if you please!

Lory — Must we listen to his story again?

Mouse — <u>I'll</u> soon make you dry. This is the driest thing I know. William the Conqueror, whose cause was favoured by the Pope, was soon...

Lory — (*Loud yawn*).

Mouse I'll proceed! The patriotic Archbishop of Canterbury found it advisable...

Lory Found what?

Mouse Found it. Of course you know what 'it' means. He found it advisable to meet William and offer him the crown. (*To Alice*). How are you getting on now, my dear?

Alice I'm as wet as ever. It doesn't seem to dry me at all.

Dodo In that case, I move that the meeting adjourn, for the immediate adoption of more energetic remedies.

Lory Speak English! I don't know the meaning of half those long words, and what's more, I don't believe you do either!

Dodo I was going to say that the best thing to get us dry would be a Caucus race.

Alice What is a Caucus-race?

Dodo Why, the best way to explain it is to do it. Here is the race-course (*he marks out a sort of a circle*) - the exact shape doesn't matter. Stand where you like, begin to run when you like, and leave off when you like.

THE CAUCUS RACE ***(Song & Dance)***

ALL

CHORUS ***In the caucus race you choose a starting place***
You can then begin and end exactly where you like.
In the caucus race you run at your own pace,
You'll be guaranteed to win a prize!

If your fur and feathers are a sorry sight,
If you're feeling cold and wet.
Come and join the race and you'll get dry,
There's no need to be upset!

CHORUS

It won't really matter how you play the game,
Make up any rules you like.
If you get it wrong, well that's OK,
Don't think anyone will mind.

CHORUS

PART TWO All this busy running gets you dry and it is funny
But it's really quite exhausting going round and round! (Repeat)

CHORUS AND PART TWO

PART THREE
Once you've started you've no worries,
There's no reason to be hurried.
Take it easy, stay light-hearted, in the caucus race.

PARTS TWO AND THREE
CHORUS, WITH PARTS TWO AND THREE

Dodo — The race is over!

All — But who has won?

Dodo — Everybody's won, and all must have prizes.

All — But who is to give the prizes?

Dodo — Why, <u>she</u> of course! (*Pointing at Alice*).

All — (*Crowding around Alice*). Prizes! Prizes! (*Alice hands round comfits*).

Mouse — She must have a prize herself, you know.

Dodo — Of course. (*To Alice*). What else have you got in your pocket?

Alice — Only a thimble.

Dodo — Hand it over here. (*Alice hands it to the Dodo*). We beg your acceptance of this elegant thimble. (*All cheer. Alice bows and takes the thimble. She turns to the Mouse*).

Alice — You promised to tell me your history, you know, and why it is you hate 'C' and 'D'.

Mouse — Mine is a long sad tale.

MOUSE'S TALE

MOUSE

Fury said to the mouse that he met in the house
"Let us both go to law, I will prosecute you.
I will prosecute you!
Come, I'll take no denial,
We must have a trial,
For really this morning I've nothing to do.
I've nothing to do".
Said the mouse to the cur,
"Such a trial, dear sir,
With no jury or judge,
Would be wasting our breath".
"I'll be judge, I'll be jury"
Said cunning old Fury,
"I'll try the whole cause and condemn you to death!"

Mouse — You are not attending!

Alice — I beg your pardon. I thought you had finished.

Mouse — I had not.

Alice — A knot? Oh, do let me help you undo it.

Mouse — I shall do nothing of the sort. You insult me by talking such nonsense!

Alice — I didn't mean it. (*Mouse starts to walk away*). Please come back and finish your story.

All — Yes, please come back! (*Mouse shakes his head and exits*).

Lory — What a pity it wouldn't stay!

Alice — I wish I had our Dinah here. She'd soon fetch it back!

Lory — And who is Dinah, if I might venture to ask the question?

Alice — Dinah's our cat. And she's such a capital one for catching mice. And oh, I wish you could see her after the birds!

Dodo — We really must be going. It's getting very late! (*Exit Lory, Dodo and creatures*).

Alice — I wish I hadn't mentioned Dinah. My dear Dinah, I wonder if I shall ever see you any more.

White Rabbit — The Duchess! The Duchess! Oh my dear paws! Oh, my fur and whiskers! She'll get me executed, as sure as ferrets are ferrets! Where can I have dropped them, I wonder? Why, Mary-Ann? What are you doing out here? Run home this moment and fetch me a pair of gloves and a fan! Quick! Now! (*Exits*).

Alice — He took me for his housemaid. How surprised he'll be when he finds out who I am. But I better take him his fan and gloves - that is, if I can find them.

Lewis Carroll — As she said this, Alice came upon a neat little house, on the door of which was a bright brass plate with the name 'W. RABBIT' engraved upon it. She hurried in without knocking, and found her way into a tiny room. Inside was a table and on it a fan and two or three pairs of tiny white kid gloves, and a little bottle.

WHAT WILL BECOME OF ME?

I've found another bottle, — ***ALICE***
It's given me a thought.
I'm sure that something strange will happen
If I can remove the cork.
I'm tired of being little
I'm sick of feeling small.
Perhaps if I should try this drink
I'll end up growing really tall.

CHORUS ***What will become of me now I wonder?*** — ***ALL***
I can't imagine what I should do.
Is this a magical spell I'm under?
Things keep happening that hardly seem true.

Much sooner than expected — ***ALL***
It happened as before,
But when she'd drunk a half of it
She wished she'd not begun at all.
Alas! It was too late then
She grew and grew some more.
In hardly any time she started
Feeling so uncomfortable.

CHORUS

My head's against the ceiling, — ***ALICE***
I can't get out the door.

I wish I hadn't drunk so much
I hope I don't grow anymore!
My foot is up the chimney
I'm kneeling on the floor.
My arm is out the window and my
Elbow's stuck against the wall.

CHORUS

Things keep happening, strange things happening, *ALICE*
Curious happenings that hardly seem true.

Lewis Carroll — Alice had grown so large that she was stuck fast inside the rabbit's house. Luckily for Alice, the little magic bottle had now had its full effect, and she grew no larger.

Alice — It was much pleasanter at home, when one wasn't always growing larger and smaller, and being ordered about by mice and rabbits. I do wonder what can have happened to me. I wonder what will happen next?

Lewis Carroll — And well might she have wondered, for Alice herself could hardly believe what happened next. Firstly, the White Rabbit came to look for his gloves and fan, but found he couldn't get in. Bill the Lizard was sent down the chimney to tackle the giant inside. Alice, with one sharp kick, sent him back up like a sky-rocket. Then, the rabbit and his friends showered Alice with a barrow-full of pebbles, which she noticed, with some surprise, were all turning into little cakes! Naturally, she tried one of them, and was delighted to find that she began shrinking directly. As soon as she was small enough she ran out of the house, and found herself safe in a thick wood.

Alice — The first thing I've got to do is to grow to my right size again; and the second thing is to find my way into that lovely garden. I think that will be the best plan.

Lewis Carroll — It sounded an excellent plan - the only difficulty was that she had not the smallest idea how to set about it. Alice looked all round her at the flowers and the blades of grass. There was a large mushroom growing near her, about the same height as herself. She stretched herself up on tiptoe, and peeped over the edge of the mushroom. Her eyes immediately met those of a large blue caterpillar.

WHO ARE YOU? (***Song & Dance***)

"Who are you?" said the caterpillar *ALL*
In such a lazy mood, he hardly bothered to stir.
Lackadaisical and laissez-faire
Was the little fella's attitude.

"Who can say?" Alice had to reply
It's been a strange old day, and I keep changing my size.
It's not easy to explain (I've tried)
But I'm really not myself today!

Caterpillar — What do you mean by that? Explain yourself!

Alice — I can't explain myself, I'm afraid, sir, because I'm not myself, you see.

Caterpillar — I don't see.

Alice — I'm afraid I can't put it more clearly, for I can't understand it myself to begin with; and being so many different sizes in a day is very confusing.

Caterpillar — It isn't!

Alice — Well, perhaps you haven't found it so yet, but when you have to turn into a chrysalis - you will some day, you know, and then after that into a butterfly - I should think you'll feel it a little queer won't you?

Caterpillar — Not a bit!

Alice — Well, perhaps your feelings may be different. All I know is, it would feel very queer to me.

Caterpillar — You? Who are you?!

"Come back here!" called the caterpillar.
(He sounded quite sincere, and so it mattered to her).
"I've got something that you ought to hear
And it's this...................... KEEP YOUR TEMPER!"

Alice — Is that all?

Caterpillar — No! So you think you're changed do you?

Alice — I'm afraid I am sir. I can't remember things as I used, and I don't keep the same size for ten minutes together.

Caterpillar — Repeat 'Father William'.

Alice — 'You are old Father William' the young man said,
'And your hair has become very white,
And yet you incessantly stand on your head,
Do you think at your age it is right'.

'In my youth' Father William replied to his son,
'I feared it might injure the brain.
But, now that I'm perfectly sure I have none,
Why, I do it again and again'.

"That's not right!" said the caterpillar
"If I can be precise, I've never listened to worse.
Not a solitary line or verse
Has the meaning that I thought it might.

Alice — Nothing's right today. I don't like changing so often, you know, but I should like to be a little larger, sir, if you wouldn't mind. Three inches is such a wretched height to be.

Caterpillar — It's a very good height indeed!

CATERPILLAR

"I don't know what is wrong with your size,
You shouldn't worry so, you shouldn't criticize.
You'll get used to being inches high,
It's the perfect height, and I should know!
Please excuse me now, I have to go! (*slowly crawls away*)

Alice	How puzzling all these things are. I'm never sure what's going to happen from one minute to another! Anyway, I've got to get into that beautiful garden - how is it to be done, I wonder?
Lewis Carroll	As she said this, Alice suddenly came upon an open place with a little house in it, about four feet high. For a minute or two she stood looking at the house, wondering what to do next, when a footman in livery came running out of the wood and went to the front door.

PIG AND PEPPER

The Queen has invited the Duchess to play	***FISH FOOTMAN***
Along with the others, a game of croquet.	
The Duchess will gladly receive from the Queen,	***FROG FOOTMAN***
An invite to join her for games on the green.	

(Both bow low, curls get entangled. Exit fish footman. Frog sits on doorstep. Alice knocks on door).

There's no point in knocking, you'll never get in,	***FROG FOOTMAN***
Besides, they're all making a terrible din!	
I will be here 'til tomorrow, for sure,	
Day after day I shall sit by the door.	
But Footman, excuse me, before you begin	***ALICE***
Please will you tell me how I can get in?	
How do you know if you'll get in at all?	***FROG FOOTMAN***
There's no use in talking to him, he's a fool!	***ALICE***

INSTRUMENTAL

The noise in the kitchen was fearfully loud.	***ALL***
The smoke from the cooking was thick as a cloud.	
The cook in the corner was using a scoop	
To stir up the pepper she'd put in the soup.	
The cat was sat grinning from ear to ear,	
The reason it did so was not very clear.	
The duchess was nursing a baby that sneezed,	
Howling and screaming it sat on her knees.	
Rock-a-bye baby sat on a stool,	***ALL (SUNG)***
Watch out for saucepans, dishes and all.	
Beat him and shake him, throw him around.	
He'll go to sleep when he hits the ground!!	

INSTRUMENTAL x2 *(Baby lobbing)*

Alice	There's certainly too much pepper in that soup! Please would you tell me why your cat grins like that?
Duchess	It's a Cheshire cat, and that's why. (*To baby*) Pig!
Alice	I didn't know that cats could grin.
Duchess	They all can, and most of them do.
Alice	I don't know of any that do.

Duchess — You don't know much, and that's a fact. (*Cook starts throwing things at Duchess*).

Alice — Please mind what you're doing! Oh, there goes his precious nose!

Duchess — If everybody minded their own business, the world would go round a great deal faster than it does.

Alice — Which would not be an advantage. You see the earth takes twenty-four hours to turn on its axis..

Duchess — Talking of axes, chop off her head!

Alice — Twenty-four hours, I think, or is it twelve?

Duchess — Oh, don't bother me! I could never abide figures. Here, you may nurse it for a bit if you like. (*Flings baby at Alice and leaves*).

Lewis Carroll — Alice carried the baby out into the open air, where it started to grunt. She told it, if it was going to turn into a pig, she'd have nothing more to do with it. It grunted again, so violently that she set the little creature down, and felt quite relieved to see it trot away into the wood.

Alice — If it had grown up, it would have made a dreadfully ugly child, but it makes rather a handsome pig, I think.

Lewis Carroll — As Alice turned round, she was a little startled to see the Cheshire Cat.

Alice — Cheshire Puss! Would you tell me, please, which way I ought to go from here.

Cheshire Cat — That depends a good deal on where you want to get to.

Alice — I don't much care where...

Cheshire Cat — Then it doesn't matter which way you go!

Alice — What sort of people live about here?

Cheshire Cat — In <u>that</u> direction, lives a hatter, and in <u>that</u> direction, lives a March hare. Visit either you like, they're both mad!

Alice — But I don't want to go among mad people!

Cheshire Cat — Oh, you can't help that, we're all mad here. I'm mad, you're mad.

Alice — How do you know I'm mad?

Cheshire Cat — You must be, or you wouldn't have come here. Do you play croquet with the Queen today?

Alice — I should like it very much, but I haven't been invited yet.

Cheshire Cat — You'll see me there. By-the-bye, what became of the baby? I nearly forgot to ask.

Alice — It turned into a pig.

Cheshire Cat — I thought it would!

Lewis Carroll — With that, the Cheshire Cat slowly vanished, beginning with the end of the tail, and ending with the grin, which remained some time after the rest of it had gone.

Alice — Well! I've often seen a cat without a grin, but a grin, without a cat! It's the most curious thing I ever saw in all my life.

WONDERLAND *(Song & Dance)*

White rabbits with strange habits
That run round in a mad panic,
Never having time to turn around.
Long hallways with small doorways
Are there sometimes, but not always,
Curious indeed - the things I've found. *ALICE*

CHORUS ***Alice, Alice, please understand,***
These are the things that happen in a wonderland. (Repeat) *ALL*

Loud sneezing and brain-teasing,
Where words take on a new meaning,
Everyone it seems must disagree.
Rude manners and bad grammar
The frog-footman, a Mad Hatter!
It's the strangest place I've ever been! *ALICE*

CHORUS

INSTRUMENTAL *(Cast join Alice in 'gathering')*

CHORUS

END OF ACT ONE

ACT TWO

ENT'RACTE

Lewis Carroll — After watching the Cheshire Cat slowly vanish, Alice set off once more. She had not gone much further before she came in sight of the house of the March Hare. She thought it must be the right house, because the chimneys were shaped like ears and the roof was thatched with fur. There was a table set out under a tree in front of the house, and the March Hare and the Hatter were having tea at it. A Dormouse was sitting between them, fast asleep. (*Alice approaches table*).

Hare & Hatter — No room! No room!

Alice — There's plenty of room! (*Alice sits down*)

Hare — Have some wine.

Alice — I don't see any wine.

Hatter — There isn't any.

Alice — Then it wasn't very civil of you to offer it.

Hare — It wasn't very civil of you to sit down without being invited.

Alice — I didn't know it was <u>your</u> table.

Hatter — Your hair wants cutting.

Alice — You should learn not to make personal remarks - it's very rude.

Hatter — Why is a raven like a writing desk?

Alice — I believe I can guess that.

Hare — Do you mean you think that you can find the answer to it?

Alice — Exactly so!

Hare — Then you should say what you mean.

Alice — I do. At least I mean what I say. That's the same thing you know.

Hatter — Not the same thing a bit! You might just as well say that "I eat what I see" is the same as "I see what I eat".

Hare — You might just as well say that "I like what I get" is the same as "I get what I like".

Dormouse — You might just as well say that "I breathe when I sleep" is the same as "I sleep when I breathe!".

Hatter	It is the same thing with you! (*They sit silent for a minute*). What day of the month is it?
Alice	The fourth.
Hatter	Two days wrong! I told you butter wouldn't suit the works! (*looking angrily at the Hare*).
Hare	It was the best butter.
Hatter	Yes, but some crumbs must have got in as well. You shouldn't have put it in with the bread-knife.
Hare	It was the best butter, you know!
Alice	What a funny watch! It tells the day of the month and doesn't tell what o'clock it is!
Hatter	Why should it? Does your watch tell you what year it is?
Alice	Of course not, but that's because it stays the same year for such a long time together.
Hatter	Which is just the case with mine.
Alice	I don't quite understand you.
Hatter	The Dormouse is asleep again. (*Pours tea on his nose*).
Dormouse	Of course, of course; just what I was going to remark myself.
Hatter	Have you guessed the riddle yet?
Alice	No - I give up. What's the answer?
Hatter	I haven't the slightest idea!

MAD AS A HATTER! **(Song & Dance)**

CHORUS ***I'm mad as a hatter!*** ***HATTER***
I've never felt better!
It's hard to believe that I'm out of my mind, but
I'm mad as a hatter!
So pass me the butter,
'Cause life is a tea-party all of the time!

He's mad as a hatter! **ALL**
He's never felt better! etc,...

HATTER	**DORMOUSE & HARE (or ALL)**
Ravens are rather like desks.	**(A riddle! A riddle!)**
Tell me if you think it's true.	**(Tell him, do tell him!)**
You won't be able to guess.	**(He'll have to tell you!)**
I've really not got a	
CHORUS	**He's mad as a hatter ....** **ALL**
It was the middle of March,	**(The middle! The middle!)**
I had a quarrel with time.	**(Yes we remember!)**

	Now he does nothing I ask, **He was a good friend of**	**(He never listens)**
	CHORUS	***ALL***
Hatter	I want a clean cup! Let's all move one place on!	
	I find it hard to explain, **Thoughts that go round in my head.** **Dormouse you're sleeping again!** **You'd better go back to**	**(A puzzle! A puzzle!)** **(No rhyme or reason)** **(Yawn. Twinkle twinkle)**

(*MH stuffs dormouse into teapot!*)

CHORUS

REPEAT CHORUS

Alice (*As she walks away*). I'll never go there again! It's the stupidest tea-party I ever was at in all my life!

Lewis Carroll Just as she said this, Alice noticed that one of the trees had a door leading right into it. Curious indeed - but in she went. She found herself at last in the beautiful garden, among the bright flower-beds and the cool fountains. A large rose-tree stood near the entrance of the garden, the roses growing on it were white, but there were three gardeners at it, busily painting them red.

Two Look out now, Five! Don't go splashing paint over me like that!

Five I couldn't help it! Seven jogged my elbow!

Seven That's right, Five! Always lay the blame on others.

Five <u>You'd</u> better not talk. I heard the Queen say only yesterday you deserve to be beheaded.

Two What for?

Seven That's none of your business, Two!

Five Yes it is his business, and I'll tell him - it was for bringing the cook tulip roots instead of onions.

Seven Well, of all the unjust things.. (*They see Alice and bow low*).

Alice Would you tell me why you are painting those roses?

Two (*In a low voice*). Why the fact is, you see Miss, this here ought ot have been a <u>red</u> rose-tree, and we put a white one in by mistake. If the Queen were to find out we should all have our heads cut off, you know. So, you see Miss, we're doing our best before she comes, to..

Five The Queen! The Queen!

THE ROYAL PROCESSION

FANFARE

Make Way! Here comes the royal procession! *ALL*
They make their entrance two by two.
They'll all be out to make an impression,
Be careful what you say and do.

FANFARE

This family has a sporting tradition ***(Clubs - Soldiers)*** ***ALL***
We're proven winners through and through.
Our bodies are in tip-top condition,
Our team will wipe the floor with you.

Our pride is in our social position. ***(Diamonds - Courtiers)*** ***ALL***
We're first to hear the royal news.
We're in with all the top politicians,
And all the gossip columns too!

I'm late! I'm late! - I'm getting in a terrible state, I'll have to hurry! ***W/RABBIT***
Better get a move on 'cause I'm running out of time!

Our fathers have a fine reputation, ***(Hearts - Children)*** ***ALL***
They're really rather well-to-do.
They've given us the best education,
And all the money we can use!

We're here to represent other nations, ***(Guests - Kings & Queens)*** ***ALL***
From Mexico to Timbuctu!
And we received the Queen's invitations
Before she even thought of you!!

FANFARE

Knave — "Make way for The King and Queen of Hearts!"

Queen — (*To Knave*) Who is this? (*Knave only bows and smiles in reply*). Idiot! What's your name, child?

Alice — My name is Alice, so please your Majesty.

Queen — (*Pointing to gardeners*). And who are these?

Alice — How should I know? It's no business of mine.

Queen — Off with her head! Off with..

Alice — Nonsense!

King — Consider, my dear, she is only a child.

Queen — (*To knave, re: gardeners*). Turn them over! (*Knave does so*). Get up! (*Gardeners jump up and start bowing*). Leave off that! You make me giddy. What have you been doing here?

Two — May it please your Majesty, we were trying to..

Queen — I see. Off with their heads!

Alice — You shan't be beheaded! (*Gardeners exit*)

Queen — Are their heads off?

Knave — Their heads are gone, if it please your Majesty.

Queen — (*to Alice*) Can you play croquet?

Alice — Yes!

Queen — Come on, then! (*exits*)

White Rabbit — It's - it's a very fine day.

Alicc — Very. Where's the Duchess?

White Rabbit — Hush, hush! (*Whispers*). She's under sentence of execution.

Alice — What for?

White Rabbit — She boxed the Queen's ears. (*Alice begins to laugh*). Oh, hush! The Queen will hear you! You see, she came rather late, and the Queen said...

Queen — (*Entering*) Get to your places!

CROQUET SONG

(Song & Dance)

ALL

It's such a lovely day for playing croquet,
Show me a better way to spend your time.
Really I have to say that life is OK,
Out on the lawn today, it's just divine!

I have been practising with my flamingo.
It's not an easy thing to keep in line.
I am delighted in the way my swing goes,
It needs some polishing, but I'll be fine.

Croquet is not so cool when you're a hedgehog!
Using us for a ball, it's so unkind.
If we don't curl up small, they'll knock our heads off!
Since they don't care at all, we'll run and hide!

This is an awful game if you're a soldier!
I've never been the same since first I tried.
I can't describe the pain in my left shoulder,
All doubled-up for days - it's such a crime!

Whenever you play croquet then your neck is on the line,
We should all be glad just to stay alive!

Queen — Stop! Stop! Stop! Now, it's about time the rest of you did some singing. You should all know the tune by now. Are the words ready yet? Good. Now, woe betide anyone who doesn't join in. Your head will be removed! Executioners, to your places!

It's such a lovely day for playing croquet,
(It's a beautiful day for a game of croquet)

Show me a better way to spend your time.
(It's a wonderful way to be spending your time)
Really I have to say that life is OK,
(Life is quite OK playing croquet!)
Out on the lawn today, it's just divine!

REPEAT LAST VERSE
Whenever you play croquet then your neck is on the line,
We should all be glad just to stay alive!
We should all be glad just to stay alive!

Queen	(*As she exits*) Off with her head! Off with her head! And, Off with his head!
Alice	They're dreadfully fond of beheading people here. The great wonder is, that there's any one left alive!
Cheshire Cat	How are you getting on?
Alice	I don't think they play at all fairly, and they all quarrel so dreadfully.
Cheshire Cat	How do you like the Queen?
Alice	Not at all! She's so extremely.... (*Queen enters*) ..likely to win, that it's hardly worth finishing the game.
King	(*as he enters*) Who are you talking to?
Alice	It's a friend of mine - the Cheshire Cat. Allow me to introduce it.
King	I don't like the look of it at all. However, it may kiss my hand if it likes.
Cheshire Cat	I'd rather not!
King	Don't be impertinent! And don't look at me like that!
Alice	A cat may look at a King.
King	Well, it must be removed. My dear, I wish you would have this cat removed.
Queen	Off with his head! (*Cheshire Cat exits*).
King	I'll fetch the executioner myself. (*Hurries off*).
Queen	Have you seen the Mock Turtle yet?
Alice	No, I don't even know what a Mock Turtle is.
Queen	It is the thing Mock Turtle soup is made from.
Alice	I never saw one, or heard of one.
Queen	Come on then, and he shall tell you his history. Gryphon! (*Enter Gryphon*). Hurry up,

	you lazy thing, and take this young lady to see the Mock Turtle. I must go back and see to some executions I have ordered. (*Walks off*).
Lewis Carroll	Alice was left alone with the Gryphon. She didn't quite like the look of the creature, but she thought it would be as safe to go on with him as to go after the Queen. They hadn't gone far before they saw the Mock Turtle, sitting sad and lonely on a little ledge of rock.
Alice	What is his sorrow?
Gryphon	(*With west country dialect*) It's all his fancy, that. He hasn't got no sorrow, you know. Come on! This here young lady, she wants for to know your history, she do.
Mock Turtle	I'll tell it to her. Sit down, both of you. Once, I was a real Turtle. When we were little we went to a school in the sea. The master was an old Turtle - we used to call him Tortoise.
Alice	Why did you call him Tortoise, if he wasn't one?
Mock Turtle	We called him Tortoise because he taught us! Why, you really are dull.
Gryphon	You ought to be ashamed of yourself for asking such a simple question.
Mock Turtle	We went to see in the school. We had the best of educations - in fact, we went to school every day.
Alice	I've been to a day-school, too.
Mock Turtle	With extras?
Alice	Yes, we learned French and Music.
Mock Turtle	And washing?
Alice	Certainly not!
Mock Turtle	Ah! Then yours wasn't a really good school. At <u>ours</u>, they had French, Music <u>and</u> washing - extra! I only took the regular course.
Alice	What was that?
Mock Turtle	Reeling and Writhing, of course, to begin with; and then the different branches of Arithmetic - Ambition, Distraction, Uglification and Derision.
Alice	And how many hours a day did you do lessons?
Mock Turtle	Ten hours the first day, nine the next, and so on.
Alice	What a curious plan.
Gryphon	That's the reason they're called lessons, because thy lessen from day to day! Anyway, that's enough about lessons, tell her something about the games now.

Mock Turtle Were you ever introduced to a lobster?

Alice I once tasted... No, never!

Mock Turtle So you can have no idea what a delightful thing a Lobster Quadrille is!

LOBSTER DANCE **(Song & Dance)**

GRYPHON AND/ OR MOCK TURTLE
(alternating every verse/two lines if both)

If you listen then I'll explain,
You'll see it's a delightful game.
Clear the jelly-fish out the way
And then we can begin.

Find a lobster and take his hand,
Dance together along the sand.
Change your partners and turn around
Then do it all again.

CHORUS ***Seals and turtles and everyone***
We're all having the best of fun!
Join the party, we've just begun,
Come on and do the lobster dance!

Hurl your lobster with all your might,
Out to sea where he's out of sight.
Don't you worry - he'll be all right,
He loves to play the game!

Turn a somersault in the sea,
(You will find it comes naturally!)
Bring your pa-rt-ner back and we
Can start it all again!

CHORUS

INSTRUMENTAL/PARTY CONGA

CHORUS TWICE

Alice Thank you, it's a very interesting dance to watch.

Gryphon Now, recite your poem for her.

Mock Turtle Would you like me to?

Alice Very much indeed.

Mock Turtle "Will you walk a little faster" said a whiting to a snail,
"There's a porpoise close behind us, and he's treading on my tail.
See how eagerly the lobsters and the turtles all advance!
They are waiting on the shingle - will you come and join the dance?
Will you, won't you, will you, won't you, will you join the dance?
Will you, won't you, will you, won't you, won't you join the dance?

Alice Thank you! If I'd been the whiting, I'd have said to the porpoise 'Keep back please, we don't want you with us'.

Mock Turtle — They were obliged to have him with them. No wise fish would go anywhere without a porpoise.

Alice — Wouldn't it really?

Mock Turtle — Of course not! If a fish came to me and told me that he was going on a journey, I should say "With what porpoise?"

Alice — Don't you mean 'purpose'?

Mock Turtle — I mean what I say.

Gryphon — Shall we try another figure of the Lobster Quadrille, or would you like the Mock Turtle to sing you a song?

Alice — Oh, a song please, if the Mock Turtle would be so kind.

Gryphon — Hm! No accounting for tastes! Sing her 'Beautiful Soup', will you old fellow?

BEAUTIFUL SOUP

This is a song that I love to recite, — ***MOCK TURTLE***
Do sing along if you choose.
I'll sing the chorus so you get it right,
It's not a difficult tune. (*Cadenza*) — ***Cadenza: MT/GRYPHON***

CHORUS ***Beau-ti-ful soup! Beau-ti-ful soup!*** — ***ALL***
Soup of the evening so green and so pleasing,
My beautiful, beautiful soup.
Beau-ti-ful soup! Beau-ti-ful soup!
Beau- - - - - - - - - -ti-ful
Beautiful, beautiful soup!

First thing for breakfast or last thing at night, — ***MOCK TURTLE***
This is my favourite food.
It can be served any way that you like,
I'll always be in the mood. (*Cadenza*) — ***Cadenza: MT/ GRYPHON***

CHORUS

Who cares for chicken or savoury rice, — ***MOCK TURTLE***
Vegetable curry or stew?
If I were offered whatever I liked,
Can you not guess what I'd choose?

Gryphon — Give us a clue!

Mock Turtle — Begins with an 's'.

Gryphon — (*Ad lib*)

CHORUS
Beau- - - - - - - - - -ti-ful
Beautiful, beautiful soup!

Voice Off — The trial's beginning!

Gryphon — Come on!

Alice — What trial is it?

Gryphon — Come on! (*Leaves with Alice. Mock Turtle left behind*)

Lewis Carroll — Alice and the Gryphon hurried off to the Court Room. Alice had never been in a court of justice before, but she had read about them in books. She was pleased to find that she knew the name of nearly everything there.

Alice — That's the judge, because of his great wig. And that's the jury-box.. and those twelve creatures, I suppose they are the jurors. What are they doing?

Gryphon — They're putting down their names for fear thy should forget them before the end of the trial.

Alice — Stupid things! I wish they'd get the trial done and hand round the refreshments!

King — Silence in the court! Herald, read the accusation!

White Rabbit — (*Trumpet blast. Unrolls scroll and reads*).
The Queen of Hearts, she made some tarts, all on a summer's day.
The Knave of Hearts, he stole those tarts, and took them quite away!

WHO STOLE THE TARTS?

KING
Who stole the tarts?
Who stole the tarts?

JURY
He did! He did!
'Twas the knave who stole the tarts!
(Repeat)

CHORUS — **KING & JURY first time/ALL on repeat**
Put him (her) in the prison and lock him (her) up, lock him up,
Put him (her) in the prison and throw away the key! **(Repeat)**

Rabbit — Not yet! Not yet! There's a great deal to come before that!

King — Call the first witness!

Rabbit — The first witness! (*Mad Hatter*)

KING
Take off your hat!
Take off your hat!

MAD HATTER
It's not mine sir!
I'm afraid it isn't mine!

Whose hat is that?
Whose hat is that?

JURY
Stolen?! Stolen?!
He has stolen someone's hat!!

CHORUS

Hatter — I'd rather finish my tea, sir!

King — You may go!

King — Give your evidence.

Cook Shan't!

KING
Who baked the tarts?
Who baked the tarts?

JURY
She did! She did!
'Twas the cook who baked the tarts!

What's in the tarts?
What's in the tarts?

COOK
Pepper! Pepper!
I put pepper in the tarts!

CHORUS

*Traditional. Adapted by Mark and Helen Johnson

King Never mind! Call the next witness!

Rabbit (*fumbling over list*) Alice!

Alice Here!

King What do you know about this business?

Alice Nothing.

King Nothing whatever?

Alice Nothing whatever.

King That's very important.

White Rabbit Unimportant, your Majesty means.

King Unimportant, of course. (*Under his breath*) Important, unimportant, unimportant, important...

Queen Oh, do be quiet and get on with it!

King Yes, of course dear.

OFF WITH HER HEAD!

Consider your verdict! ***KING***
Let the jury consider their verdict!

No! No! No! ***QUEEN***
(No! no! no!, No! no! no!) ***HALF JURY/OTHER HALF***
Sentence first, and the verdict afterwards! ***QUEEN***

Stuff and nonsense! ***ALICE***
The very idea of the sentence first!

Hold your tongue! ***QUEEN***
Hold your tongue! ***JURY***

I won't!! ***ALICE***

Off with her head! ***QUEEN***

	Off with her head! **Off with her head!**	***HALF JURY*** ***WHOLE JURY***
	Off with her head! **Off with her head!** **Off with her head!**	***ALL***
	Off....with her.....OFF WITH HER HEAD!!	

Alice	Who cares for you? You're nothing but a pack of cards!
Lewis Carroll	At this, the whole pack rose up into the air, and came flying down upon her. She gave a little scream, half of fright and half of anger, and tried to beat them off. She found herself on the bank, with her head in the lap of her sister, who was gently brushing away some dead leaves that had fluttered down from the trees upon her face.
Sister	Wake up, Alice dear! Why, what a long sleep you've had!
Alice	Oh, I've had <u>such</u> a curious dream!

WONDERLAND (Reprise)

Fierce ladies with pig babies, **And strange games played in weird places.** **How can I describe the things I've seen?** **Mad juries, the Queen's fury,** **The Mock-Turtle, and sad stories.** **How can I believe it's just a dream?**	***ALICE***
CHORUS ***Alice, Alice, please understand,*** ***These are the things that happen in a wonderland. (Repeat)***	***ALL***

END OF PLAY

IMPORTANT INFORMATION

It is a legal requirement for schools, nurseries, churches and all other organisations to obtain a licence from the publishers to perform musicals or plays. PRS licences and CCL licences do not cover such performances.

To simplify matters we issue affordable licences on behalf of our writers that enable you to perform the works that we publish. Our 2002/3 licence fees for 'Alice - The Musical' start at £23.50 including VAT (£20.00 in non-EU countries) for a single performance to audiences up to 100.

For your convenience you can use this form to apply for a licence. Simply photocopy this form, complete the details below and return it to Out of the Ark Music.

....

Application For A Licence To Perform 'Alice - The Musical'

Name of school / organisation: ....

Address of school / organisation: ....
....
....
....

Post Code ....
Country ....

Contact telephone number: ....

Number of performances (excl. dress rehearsals) ....
Date(s) of performance(s) ....
Average audience size of each performance ....
Will words of songs be printed in programmes? ....
Will an admission charge be made? ....
If so, please give details of ticket prices ....

Name of organiser / producer ....
Daytime telephone number ....

Will you record the show? Yes / No
Sound recording? Yes / No Number of recordings / copies ......
Video recording? Yes / No Number of recordings / copies ......

....

This form should be sent to Out of the Ark Music either by post or by fax.
Do not send payment with this form. An invoice will be issued with your licence.

Out of the Ark Music

Sefton House
2 Molesey Road
Hersham Green
Walton-on-Thames
Surrey KT12 4RQ
United Kingdom

Fax: (UK): 01932 703 010
Fax: (International): +44 1932 703 010
Tel: (UK): 01932 232 250
Tel: (International): +44 1932 232 250

E-mail: music@outoftheark.com
Web Site: www.outoftheark.com

NOTES

NOTES

NOTES

edexcel
advancing learning, changing lives

Edexcel DiDA

Diploma in Digital Applications

Graphics

Pat Tilley
Martin Gillies

Contents

Introduction

Welcome to Graphics

Congratulations! Now you have completed Unit 1, and maybe other units of the Diploma in Digital Applications (DiDA), and you are ready to move on to Unit 3.

Unit 3 lets you get to grips with the use of ICT to communicate messages in a wide range of different contexts. You have already done a lot of the groundwork for this unit in Unit 1. You will find the practical hands-on approach stimulating and rewarding.

This unit will provide you with the skills you need to design and create effective graphic products. To start with you will investigate existing products to find out how images are used to convey a particular message. Then you will learn how to design and produce your own graphics that work effectively on screen and in print. Finally, you will bring all the elements you have collected together to create graphic products.

You will demonstrate your graphics skills by working on a project set by Edexcel. You will exhibit this in an eportfolio, which will be a graphic product in itself.

You can find out more by looking at the specification on Edexcel's website.

A reminder about DiDA

- **Award in Digital Applications (AiDA):** If you've already successfully completed Unit 1, you are eligible for this. It is equivalent to one GCSE.
- **Certificate in Digital Applications (CiDA):** Successfully completing Unit 1 and Unit 3 (or any one of the other optional units) entitles you to this award. It is equivalent to two GCSEs.
- **Diploma in Digital Applications (DiDA):** If you successfully complete Unit 1 and *three* optional units you are eligible for DiDA. It is equivalent to four GCSEs.

At the moment the optional units are *Unit 2: Multimedia*, *Unit 3: Graphics* and *Unit 4: ICT in Enterprise*, but others may be added in the future.

Audience and purpose

One of the key themes in Unit 1 was the importance of producing publications that are right for the intended audience. This is just as important for graphic products. So how do you do this?

The key questions you need to ask yourself are:

- **Who** is it for?
- **Why** is it needed?
- **Where** is the audience?
- **What** must go in it?

Answering these questions will help you to identify exactly what you are trying to achieve. Once you've done this you can *then* decide:

- **How** you are going to go about it.

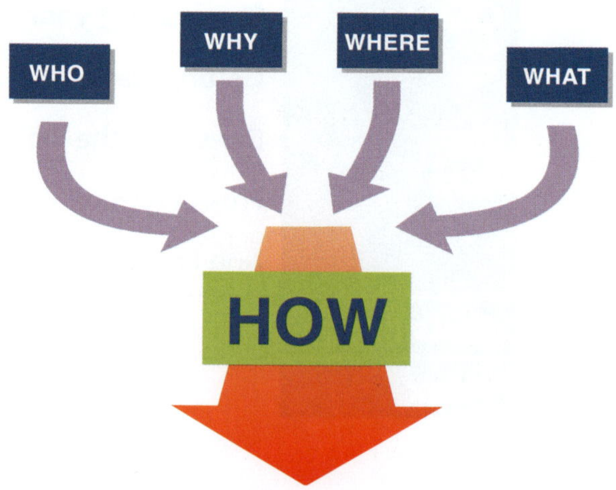

Think carefully before you decide how

How to use the ActiveBook

DiDA is all about digital applications and these materials reflect this. As well as the printed book there is also an ActiveBook. This is on the CD that comes with the book, and you may also be able to view it over your centre's network.

The ActiveBook is a digital version of the paper-based book. The pages look the same, but there is a big difference – it's interactive!

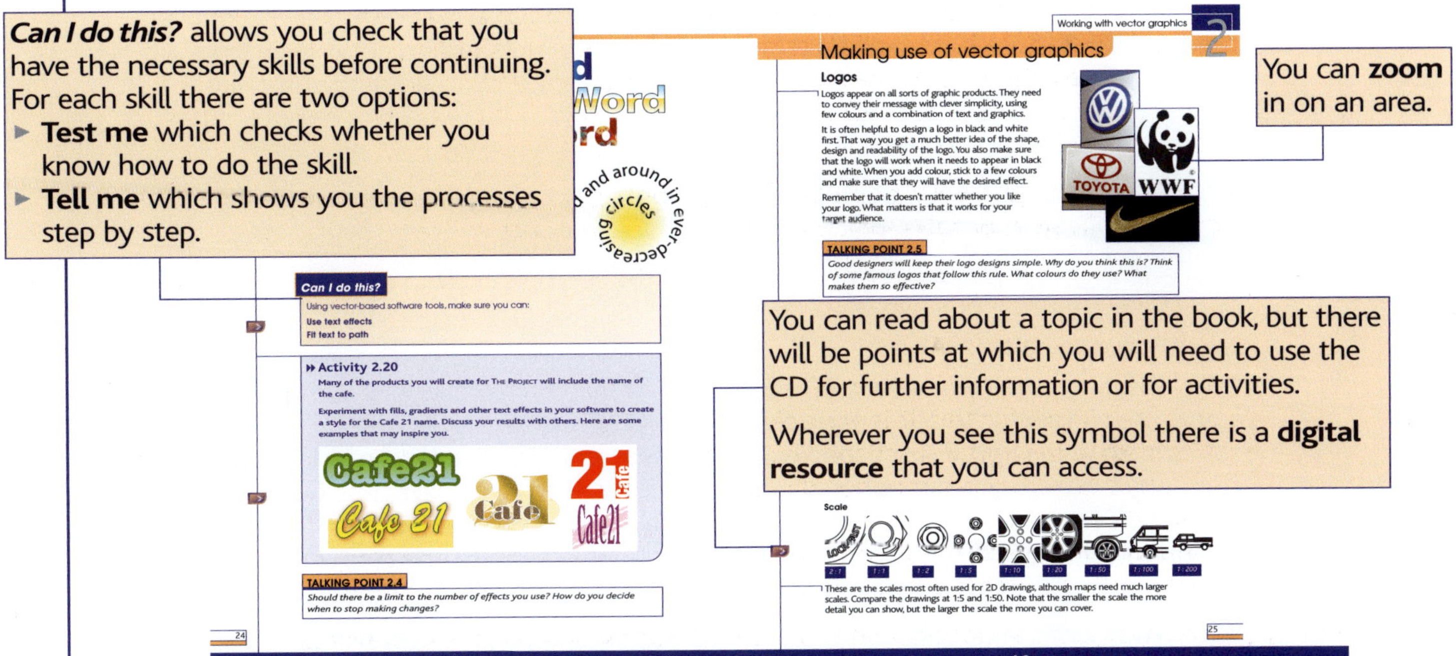

Go to these pages in the ActiveBook and try out these functions for yourself.

If you are looking at the ActiveBook on a network you will also be able to watch the **digimodules** – these are introductory presentations at the start of each chapter.

Assessment

You will remember from Unit 1, and any other DiDA units you have done, that there is no formal exam. Instead you work on a project. The project is described in the Summative Project Brief (SPB), which is published as a website by Edexcel. It gives you the chance to demonstrate the skills you have gained in the unit by developing graphic products that are creative, effective and fit for purpose. The final stage of the SPB is to create an eportfolio that will allow others to view your publications on screen and to see evidence of how you produced them.

Preparing for the SPB

THE PROJECT is a mini website just like the real SPB. It has the same type of structure and content. You will find it on the CD or on your network. It lets you practise planning and producing graphic products. Then, just like the SPB, you will showcase what you have done and how you did it in an eportfolio.

The final page in each chapter is called TACKLING THE PROJECT. These will guide you through each stage of completing THE PROJECT.

Good luck and enjoy the course!

1 Investigating graphic products

Look around you. Wherever you are, you will be surrounded by graphics. When you log on to websites, play computer games, travel from place to place or go shopping, you will see graphics at work.

Think about all the different types of graphic products you see when you go to the supermarket – signs to show you where the cafe, exit and toilets are; posters to attract your attention to special offers; and packaging that makes you want to buy a product.

Some graphics are so familiar that you probably don't even notice them, like the sign used for a bus stop or train station. Many clothing companies put their logo on their products, especially on sports and leisure clothing and footwear, making the wearer a walking advertisement for them.

You need to become 'graphic-aware'. Investigate and evaluate as many graphic products as you can. What are they trying to tell you? Notice what works and what doesn't. Pick up some tricks of the trade to help you develop your own graphic products.

In this chapter you will learn about:

- ***graphic products and what they are used for***
- ***different types of graphic elements***
- ***how graphic elements are combined on products***
- ***how graphic elements are used to create visual links and brands***

What is a graphic product?

What exactly is a graphic product? Not surprisingly, the emphasis is on the use of graphics to get a message across.

TALKING POINT 1.1

Look at how graphics are used on these products. Would the products work without them? Who is the target audience for each product? What message do the graphics convey?

Graphic products are made up of different components called graphic elements. The elements are combined together to create the overall effect.

The main elements on the front of this CD packaging are the background photograph, the combined image of flag and fireworks, the main title and secondary text. A lot of thought has gone into the positioning of elements and the use of colour to create the right effect.

TALKING POINT 1.2

Does the front cover attract attention? Why do you think each element has been chosen? Why have the elements been positioned in this way?

The back cover of the CD packaging is just as important, but for different reasons. It does not need to attract attention but it does need to give important information.

TALKING POINT 1.3

As the back cover of the packaging can't be seen in the shop, does the design matter? What has the designer done to make the two sides work together? What elements appear on the back cover?

Maps, diagrams, patterns, cartoons and plans are also graphic elements. The design of each element and the way elements are positioned and combined on the product need careful planning. The challenge is to combine the elements effectively to create attractive products that are fit for purpose.

▸▸ Activity 1.1

Collect examples of graphic products – or take photographs if that is easier. What is the target audience for each product? Make a list of the main elements used in each design. For each element, comment on its position and size within the overall design.

Types of graphic product

Let's look at the different types of graphic product in more detail. What are they used for? How are they designed to be suitable for their purpose? What audience are they aimed at?

Packaging

Product packaging such as a gift bag or a box is often a graphic product. It can display the contents, a logo and text. You can probably think of other elements you would expect to see, such as a barcode. The packaging may be made from paper, card, plastic or fabric.

Many packages are folded from flat shapes called nets. The various elements need to be positioned accurately on the net to achieve the desired effect.

Look at the net used to make this box.

Most packages will be regularly shaped as this makes them easy to store. Some packages will use shape to reinforce their purpose, as shown by this chocolate box.

⏩ Activity 1.2

Which of the graphic products you collected is made from a net? Choose one and take it apart to see how it works.

Magazines

Every magazine has its own audience and style. Magazines such as *Vogue* and *Elle* are called 'glossies' because they contain high-resolution colour images printed on glossy paper. In contrast, an image in a newspaper may be printed in black and white on recycled paper.

Brochures

Think about what you need from a holiday brochure: to book a holiday you need to know what the destination looks like, the available dates and cost of the holiday, the facilities and local attractions. This information must be presented in a way that will make people want to book the trip. It can only be achieved using graphic elements including images and charts as well as text.

⏩ Activity 1.3

Collect some examples of magazines and brochures. Look at the design of each example. What works well? What is less successful?

Signs

Signs use graphic elements to give information often with few words. They can tell you where to find a bus stop or a train station. Some are really important – to stop a driver going the wrong way down a one way street or to warn people of potential dangers. They need to be understood quickly, sometimes by people who speak a different language.

TALKING POINT 1.4

Look at these examples. Do you know what the symbols mean? Are they unambiguous? Are colours used to help convey the messages? Is the shape of the sign significant?

▸▸ Activity 1.4

Look at the Think! Road Safety website. It tells you what types of signs are used to give information to motorists. Sketch two signs indicating that an area is safe for children to play in. Aim one at motorists and one at young children.

Posters

Posters can be as big as a building or as small as A4. They can be printed or digital. This video clip shows some digital posters on the London Underground.

The content and the number of graphic elements will depend on the poster's purpose and target audience. A poster is likely to concentrate on a single topic and will often need to use text clearly to convey important details such as names or dates.

TALKING POINT 1.5

Sometimes a simple idea can be the most effective. Look at this example of a poster displayed in the window of a sandwich shop that specialises in natural, freshly-made food. Why do you think they used this image? Does it work for you?

▸▸ Activity 1.5

Images are almost always the most important elements on posters. Find examples of posters which rely on images to get their message across.

Digital stories

Digital stories are viewed and read on screen. They offer great opportunities for the use of illustrations, both still and moving. Some digital stories have no text at all. Have a look at this example.

Websites

Every website is a graphic product and is likely to include a number of different types of graphic element.

TALKING POINT 1.6

Look at this screen. What different types of graphic element can you spot? What can you tell about the target audience from the style of the graphic elements used?

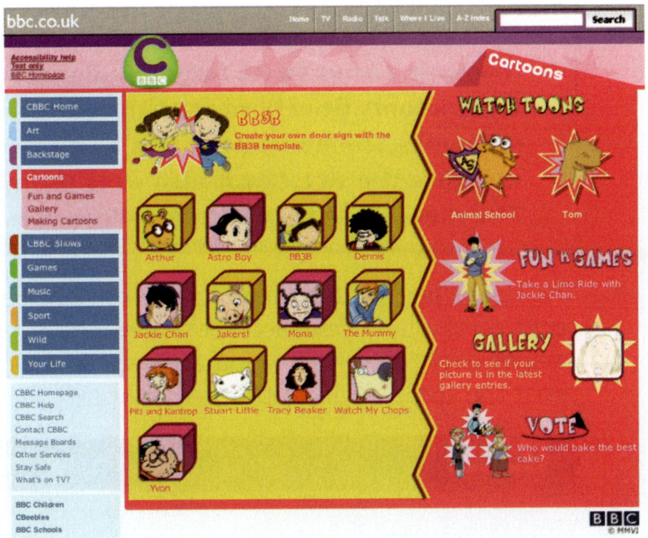

In addition to common graphic elements such as logos, text, photographs and symbols, a website can include elements designed specifically for the web such as animations, banners and buttons.

▸▸ Activity 1.6

Look at these websites. How are graphic elements used on the home pages? What is the purpose of the graphic elements?

▸▸ Activity 1.7

Look at the Wall's website. What is its purpose? Who is its target audience? Contrast this with the support section of the Apple website and answer the same questions. How do the graphic elements, and their use, differ on these websites?

Thumbnail web images are small so that a range of other images, such as products in an online store, can be shown too. A thumbnail image also entices the user and suggests what the image will be like when made larger. Clicking on thumbnail images usually results in a larger version of the image 'popping up'.

Activity 1.8

Visit the Disney website and explore it to see how the company gets its message across to its target audience. Disney is all about colour, fun, animation and pictures (much more than words) and this site makes good use of these elements. The home page has a conventional set of buttons allowing you to navigate the site, but it also uses thumbnails to represent each area of the site. The message is that Disney online is as exciting as the 'real' Disney.

The home page of the Ladybird books website encourages you to 'explore' it by using the spots on the ladybird. Each spot takes you to a different section of the site. Although the images don't always give you an idea of what to expect, they are fun and it's difficult to resist the temptation to try them all out!

TALKING POINT 1.7

Ladybird could have used images of their books to illustrate this page. Why do you think they chose not to? Are the graphic elements effective?

Activity 1.9

Sketch out ideas for a new home page for the DiDA microsite. Think about the audience and purpose when planning the elements, colour, positioning and visual effects. Pay particular attention to the form of navigation used.

Looking at graphic elements

Every graphic product is different. What makes a product work? How do the graphic elements work together to convey a message? The possibilities are endless.

The way in which graphic elements are combined in terms of size, position and prominence determines the impact, and level of success, of a product. Just changing one aspect of an element can completely alter the effect of a product.

Colour

A company may use one or more particular colours in its logo, on its packaging and in its shops. Colour can also be used to give a message: for example, black and gold suggest 'sophistication' and green could mean 'natural' or 'fresh'. Look at some examples of a supermarket's food ranges to see how colour can be used. What colours does the company use for its range of organic products?

Images

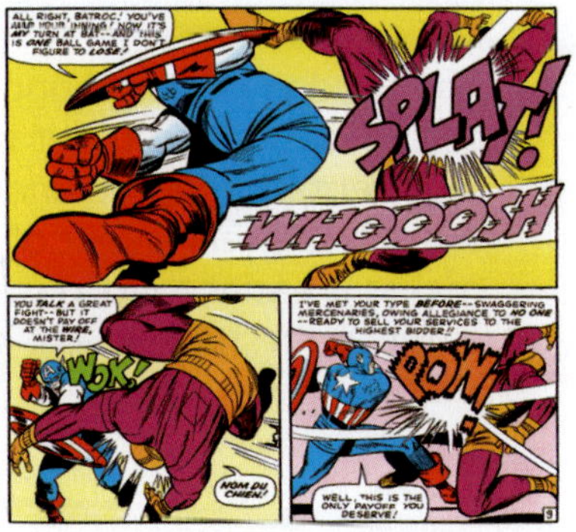

Images appear on most graphic products. Look at any magazine, newspaper, poster or website and you will see different types of images. For example, comics mainly use cartoons (either hand-drawn or computer art) to tell a story. Websites use all of these different types of image to get their message across. Each image is used to give information to a target audience in a particular way.

Photographs are particularly useful when a clear picture is needed. Fashion magazines and catalogues are full of photographs showing the latest make-up and clothes. The colours must be accurate to avoid complaints.

⏩ Activity 1.10

Look through a magazine and a newspaper and make a list of all the different images used. Think about why each type of image is used. How does the use of images in the magazine differ from the newspaper?

Symbols

You have already looked at a number of symbols used on signs. Symbols give a lot of information, frequently without any words. They tell you which way to hold a box so that the contents don't get damaged. They warn you that the contents of a bottle are dangerous. They help you find the exit in an emergency.

A good symbol is simple with a clear outline. If colour is used it will be strong and bright.

TALKING POINT 1.8

How many other examples of symbols can you think of? What type of graphic product does each appear on? What message does it convey? Why does it work?

Maps

A map can be anything from a simple sketch to a detailed representation of an area such as provided by the Ordnance Survey. Road maps are drawn to scale so that you can work out distances; in other maps scale is not nearly as important.

▸▸ Activity 1.11

What types of graphic elements are used in maps?

A map can be a graphic product in its own right or it can be part of another product. Can you think of graphic products where a map is one of the elements? How important is scale in each example?

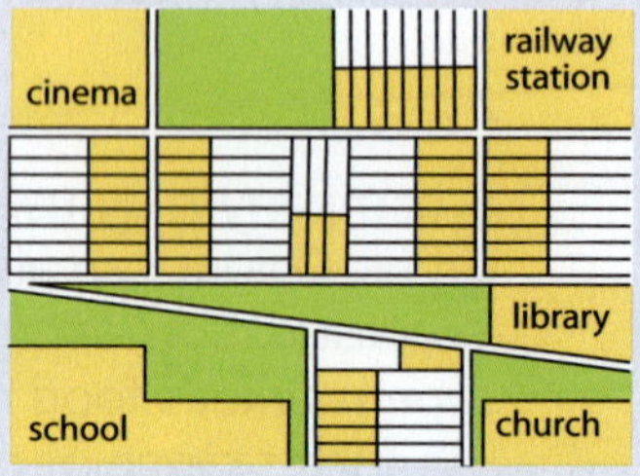

The London Underground map is considered a design classic because it is an effective representation of the underground network. It distorts the real layout of the network, but this makes it easier to follow and therefore fit for purpose. Its shape is also suitable for a poster or leaflet.

▸▸ Activity 1.12

Visit the Transport for London website to see a demonstration of how the tube map differs from the real underground network.

Plans

Plans are usually drawn to scale to ensure that the finished product is the correct size and shape. Imagine what could have happened to the Channel Tunnel if the engineers had used inaccurate plans!

TALKING POINT 1.9

Look at this floor plan for a house. What can you learn about the house from this plan?

TALKING POINT 1.10

Using the plan for information, can you work out what the front and back of the house might look like?
When might a plan appear as one element on a graphic product rather than as a product in its own right?

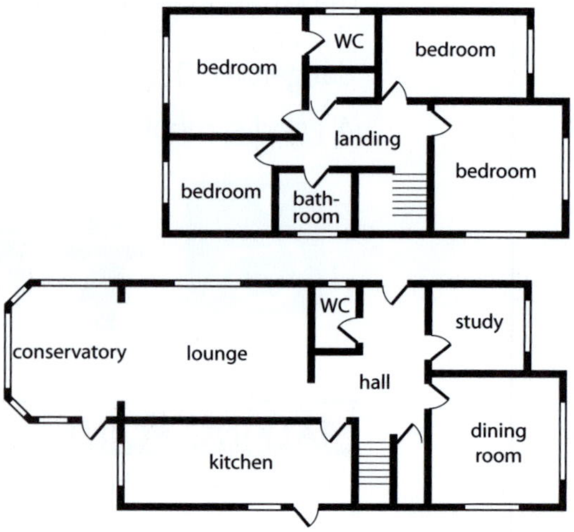

Diagrams

Have you ever tried to make a model from a kit? Written instructions might say 'Insert part A into hole B making sure that side D is the correct way up'. Such a description can be very difficult to visualise – a diagram is a much more helpful way of showing you exactly how all the parts fit together. Good diagrams often contain some text describing the objects in the diagram.

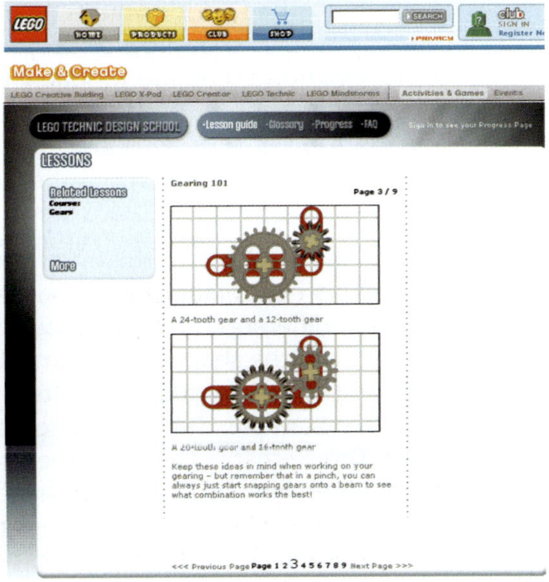

▶▶ Activity 1.13

Try following these instructions to make a paper aeroplane.

First take a rectangular A4 sheet of paper and fold down the centre lengthways, opening it out again afterwards. Take the first 1 cm and fold it up along the dotted line. Fold the flap over and over until about $\frac{3}{8}$ of the length of the sheet is folded in this concertina fashion. This should give a heavy and thick front lip. Now fold the top two corners so that the top edges lie along the centre line. Fold along the centre line. Fold the wings down so that they are horizontal.

This would be so much easier with some diagrams!

Branding

How do you find your favourite brand of baked beans in the supermarket? Do you carefully read all the labels or do you look for the colour, shape and font of the label? The company knows that you probably use the second method. It wants to make sure that you can recognise its products because if you like its beans, you might try its soup or ketchup too. For this method to work at least some of the graphic elements on the packaging of different products, such as font, colour and logo, must be consistent.

Look at the products to the right. Some elements on each label are the same and some are different. The label colour is different but the shape is the same. Because we have seen the products so often we know, for example, that 'turquoise' means beans. The elements that stay the same, such as the company name, are always positioned in the same place on the label, making it easy for you to spot these products on the shelf.

Many organisations use graphic elements to represent their brands. These are designed to provide visual links between products, but most importantly they are intended to be instantly recognisable.

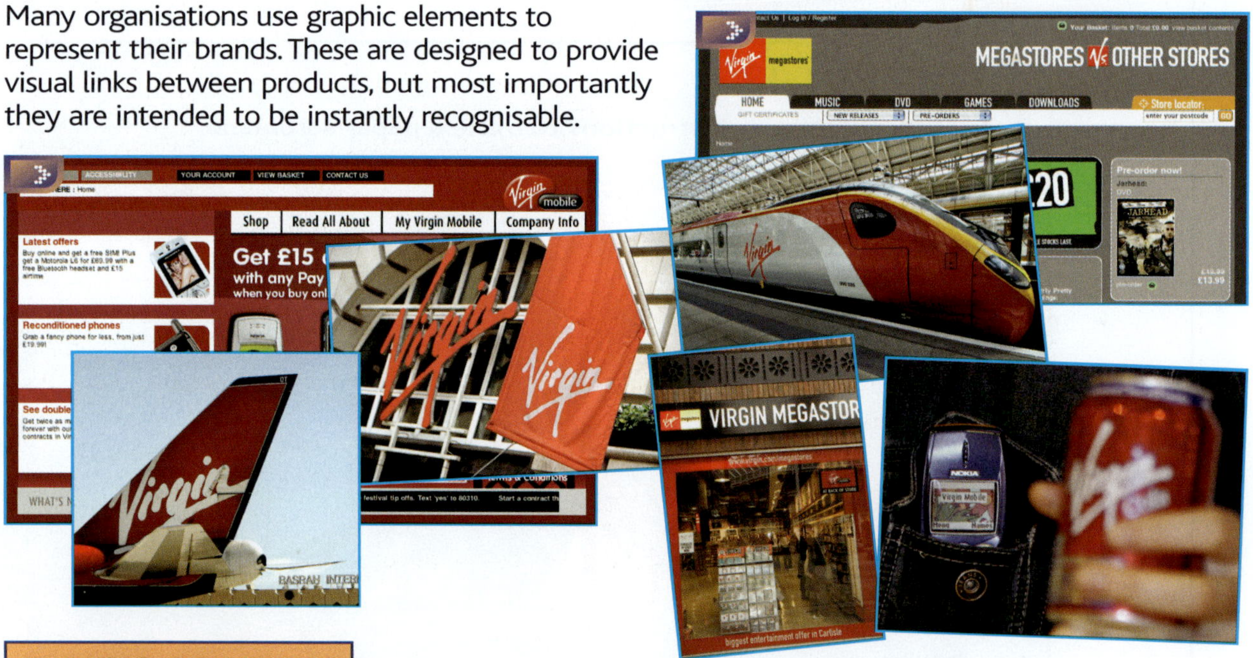

TALKING POINT 1.11

Can you think of other examples where graphic elements are used to make a brand instantly recognisable and to make visual connections between products? What graphic elements are used to provide these links?

Activity 1.14

Check out your local supermarket or your cupboards at home. Look at some graphic products and elements made by the same company. What do they have in common? What are the differences?

Logos

A logo is a type of symbol used to represent a brand and to promote products or services. Just about everything you buy has the company's logo on the packaging and sometimes on the product itself.

Good design and consistent use of a logo can make a huge difference to the success of a company or enterprise.

TALKING POINT 1.12

Companies often spend lots of money developing a distinctive logo. Why do you think this is? For each of these well-known logos, think about what may have influenced the design.

A logo can be used as a graphic product in its own right – such as the use of the McDonald's 'M' as a sign. This logo is also used in combination with other graphic elements on other products such as clothing, packaging, posters and advertisements. You see the logo – you know the brand.

Creating an impression

What is a company trying to say about itself? For example, 'we are a cutting-edge company selling state-of-the-art products' or 'we are an old family firm selling traditional products'. The packaging on these two products is clearly aimed at different markets, but how is the message conveyed?

Tackling THE PROJECT

P

THE PROJECT is similar to a real Unit 3 SPB but there are three main differences:

- You will work on sections of **THE PROJECT** as you complete each chapter. For the real SPB you will have at least 30 hours to do the whole project in one go.
- You don't have to produce a complete project plan for **THE PROJECT** because you are told when to tackle each section.
- There are more products in **THE PROJECT** than in the real SPB.

Open **THE PROJECT** and read each of the pages to make sure that you understand what you are being asked to do, especially the requirements for each graphic product.

Investigating similar products

Look for good examples of the types of product you are going to design.

For each one, identify the target audience and the purpose. What types of graphic element have been used? How have they been combined?

Look out for related products and how colours and common elements have been used to create visual links.

When you see good ideas that you want to use in your own products, keep a record of them.

Create a directory folder

At this point you should create a directory folder structure so that you can organise files as you create them. This will make it easier to find them when you need them. You will require some, but not all, of these files for your eportfolio. You should also be thinking about the structure and content of your eportfolio from the outset.

2 Working with vector graphics

Many pieces of artwork that you see in print or on screen these days are vector graphics. Vectors are used to create drawings, maps, plans and logos, among other things. They are good for scale drawings, such as the net for a box or gift bag.

Vectors are line drawings, but they need not be plain or boring. They can be filled with colour, enhanced with patterns, and made to look realistic with textures, tones and lighting effects. A good vector drawing can look almost like a photograph, or it can be as plain as it needs to be to achieve its purpose.

Using vectors allows you to draw accurately. The drawings can then be enlarged or reduced without any loss of quality, which is useful if you want to use a logo on a carrier bag as well as on the side of a truck!

In this chapter you will learn how to create and edit vector graphics by:

- ***working with lines and shapes***
- ***adding colours and other effects***
- ***working with text***
- ***applying special effects***
- ***using layers and combining vectors***

2

Vector graphics

The good news is that you don't have to be an artist to create really good vector drawings! Vector graphics are produced using lines and simple shapes. This vector drawing of a boat is a good example.

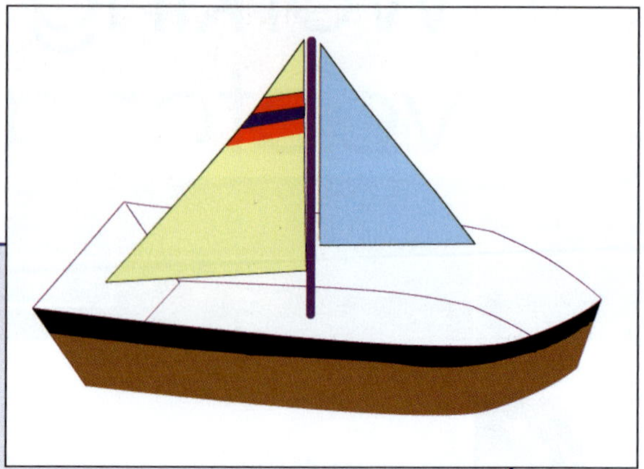

⏩ Activity 2.1

Watch this animation to see how the drawing of a boat was built up using lines and simple shapes. How many shapes can you spot?

Believe it or not, this scene was also created using vector tools. Look at how colours and patterns have been used to fill the various shapes.

TALKING POINT 2.1

What else has been done to make this picture so effective?

⏩ Activity 2.2

Collect some examples of drawings and pictures that you think were produced using vector tools. Are they effective? What shapes can you see in the drawings?

What are vectors good for?

Vector tools are good for producing any sort of drawing, for example:

- plans and elevations to show views of 3D objects
- charts and diagrams to illustrate results of data analysis or experiments
- maps to represent an area to scale
- logos to identify organisations or brands
- buttons and banners to enhance websites.

TALKING POINT 2.2

One of the advantages of vector graphics is that they can be resized without losing quality. When might this be important?

Shapes

Straight or curved?

Shapes that have straight edges are called polygons. Your vector-based software will have tools for producing polygons. All you have to do is tell the computer how many edges you want and how long you want them to be. If you want to draw a regular polygon where all the edges are the same length, you can draw one edge to set the length and let the computer do the rest. Circles and ellipses have one continuous curved edge. You can use an ellipse (oval) tool to draw them.

Strokes and fills

The outline of a shape is called the stroke. You can define the properties of the stroke, such as its thickness or colour. The shape can be filled with colour. This fill can be controlled separately from the stroke.

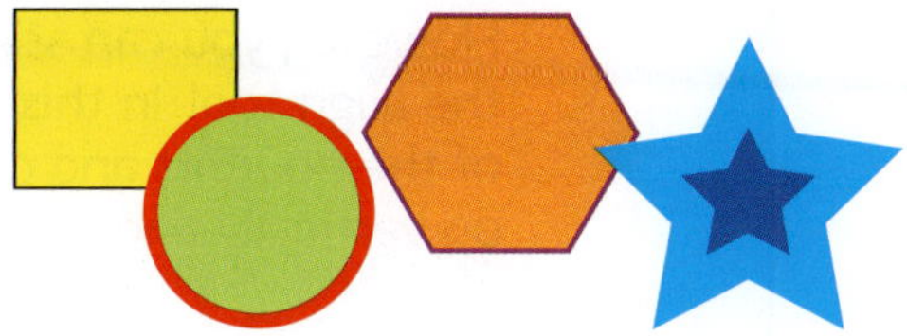

Lines

Most drawings will need lines as well as shapes. They can be straight or curved, any thickness, any length and any colour you like. They can also be continuous or broken.

Can I do this?

Using vector-based software tools, make sure you can:

- **Draw lines, curves and basic shapes**
- **Alter the thickness of the stroke**
- **Paint the stroke separately**
- **Add fills**

Activity 2.3

Explore your vector graphic software and find out which basic shapes it will create for you. Draw your own versions of the shapes shown above. Use a variety of line types and thicknesses and experiment with other properties.

Activity 2.4

Using only basic vector shapes, create a simplified version of this drawing. The drawing should be 100 mm × 150 mm and suitable for use in a book aimed at children aged 4 to 7. Use colours to make it more interesting.

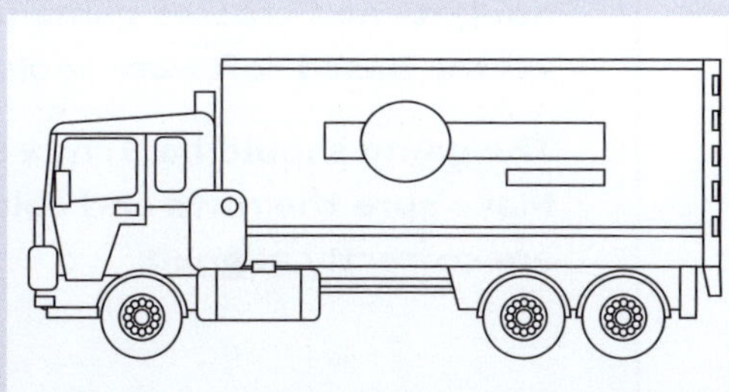

Tools and techniques

There are lots of different vector tools. We are going to look at some of the most useful, but you should explore your software to see what else is available.

Grids

Grids help you to align objects in a vector drawing. Using a grid is like drawing on graph paper. You can use an option called 'Snap to the grid', which means that each new line or shape will be forced to start at the nearest intersection point of the grid. You can set the scale of the grid for greater accuracy.

Alignment

To give you more flexibility, you may want to turn off the snap to grid function. However, you can still align images using the align tool. In this example, the centres of the noughts and crosses have been lined up vertically and horizontally.

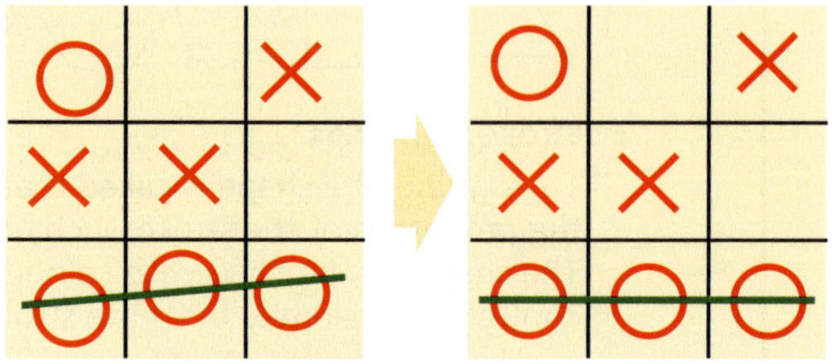

Order

You can control the order of the objects from front to back. In the noughts and crosses game the move forward option has been used to bring the winning line to the front.

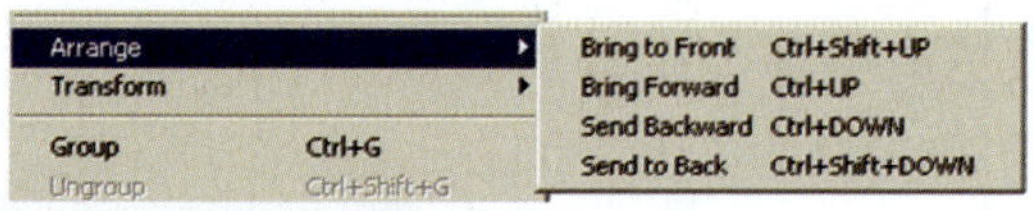

You can make objects appear closer or more important by making their outlines thicker than the outlines of other objects. Lines can also be colour coded as on this road map.

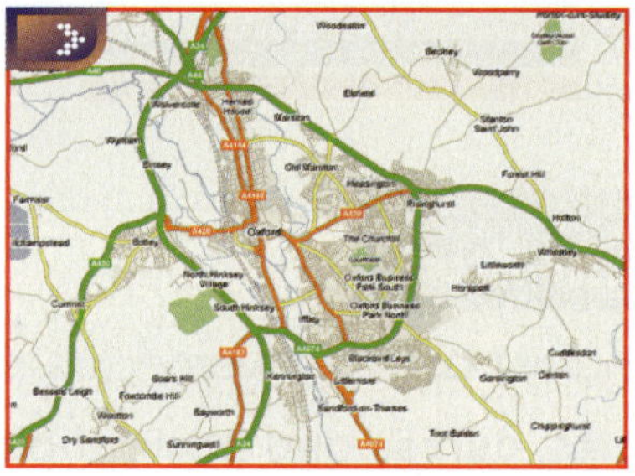

Can I do this?

Using vector-based software tools, make sure you can:

Align objects
Use grids
Cut, copy and paste

▸▸ Activity 2.5

Create a drawing of a completed noughts and crosses game using vector-based software tools.

The game should be 9 cm x 9 cm. Make sure the rows and columns are correctly aligned.

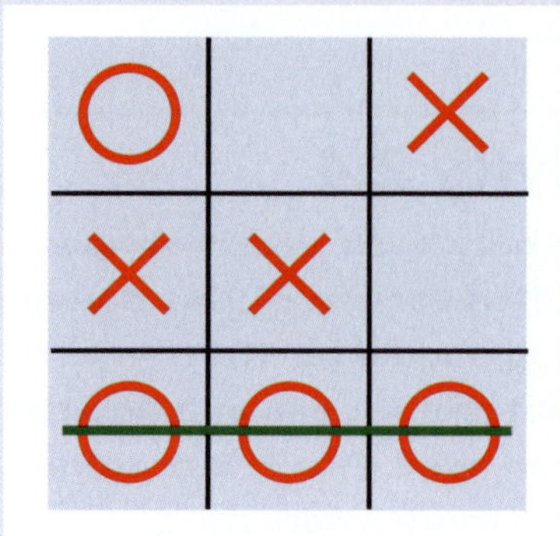

Group, ungroup and regroup

⏩ Activity 2.6

Experiment with your drawing of the noughts and crosses game. What happens to the other objects if you move one of the crosses?

Is it easy to change the size of the game? How can you make the whole drawing bigger or smaller? Try moving the whole drawing to a different position on the screen.

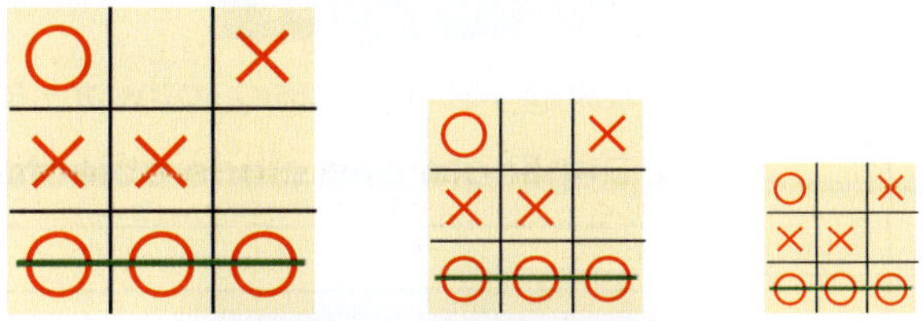

The problem is that your drawing consists of a number of separate lines and shapes. If the separate objects are not grouped together, each object has to be moved or resized individually. If you want to manipulate the complete drawing, you first need to group the items together.

If you need to make changes to parts of the drawing, for example if you want to replace a nought with a cross, you must first ungroup it. Then you can work on any line or shape as you did at the beginning. Once you have finished editing, you can regroup the drawing.

Can I do this?

Using vector-based software tools, make sure you can:

Group and ungroup objects

⏩ Activity 2.7

Group the objects in your noughts and crosses game. Move the complete game to a different position on the screen – if any objects are left behind you have not successfully grouped it! Resize the game to 12 cm × 12 cm.

Alter the result of the game by changing some of the crosses to noughts and vice versa. You will need to ungroup it. Regroup it and check that it is one complete object.

Rotate

It is more accurate to rotate a shape than to try and draw it in the required position. Here, the game has been rotated by 45 degrees. The rotation tool allows you to specify the angle. A rotation of 180 degrees produces a reflection or mirror image of an object.

Rotate is likely to be only one of a range of tools provided by your software for modifying objects.

⏩ Activity 2.8

Try rotating your noughts and crosses game by different degrees.

Can I do this?

Using vector-based software tools, make sure you can:

Rotate objects

Duplicate and clone

If you need more than one copy of an object, it is much more accurate to allow the software to do this for you. Cloning places a copy of an object on top of the original for you to position. Duplicating places a copy of an object close to the original – you decide where. It is possible to add a rotation to a duplicate command, for example each new object could be rotated a further 45 degrees.

Can I do this?

Using vector-based software tools make sure you can:

Duplicate and clone objects

▸▸ Activity 2.9

This drawing of a computer workstation has been produced using vector software tools. The objects have been grouped.

Reduce the size of the workstation by 50% and copy it.

Align the two images and then copy it again so that you have four workstations.

Rotate and reposition two of the workstations to create a back-to-back arrangement of four, as shown opposite.

Try to copy the positions of the various objects at each workstation (you will need to ungroup and regroup).

Crop and trim objects

You will sometimes want to use just part of a vector drawing. Cropping allows you to select a section and delete it. You can also trim the edges off lines to tidy up a drawing.

Can I do this?

Using vector-based software tools, make sure you can:

Crop and trim objects

▸▸ Activity 2.10

Crop your drawing from Activity 2.9 so that only half of the two lower workstations is visible.

Combine and break apart objects

Simple shapes can be combined to produce another object. In this drawing the combine tool has been used to create a new shape from a circle and a rectangle.

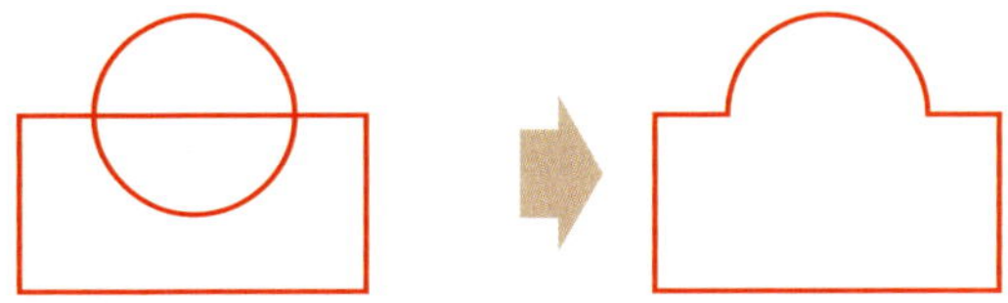

In this drawing a new object has been produced from the intersection of the two circles.

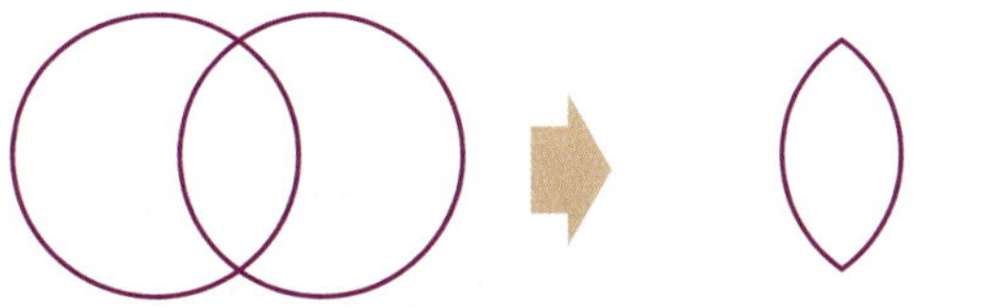

You can also break vector drawings apart to form a number of simpler objects.

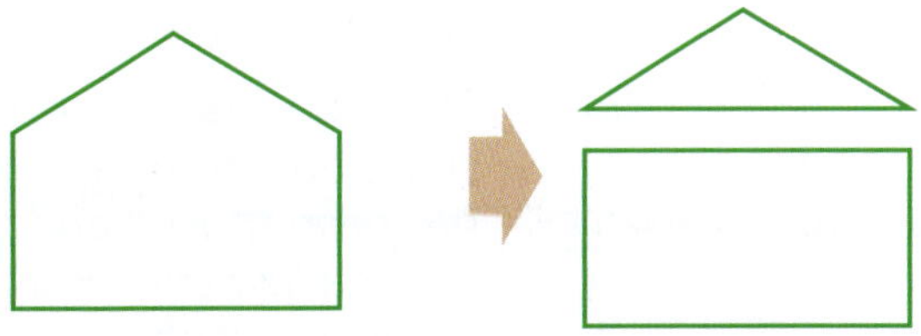

Can I do this?

Using vector-based software tools, make sure you can:

Combine and break apart objects | **Cut and join shapes**

▸▸ Activity 2.11

Explore your vector software and experiment with tools that allow you to combine and break apart vector objects.

Freehand drawing

The freehand tool allows you to draw anything you like. It allows you to be creative, but it is one of the most difficult vector tools to use well. Your software may help by smoothing out minor inaccuracies for you.

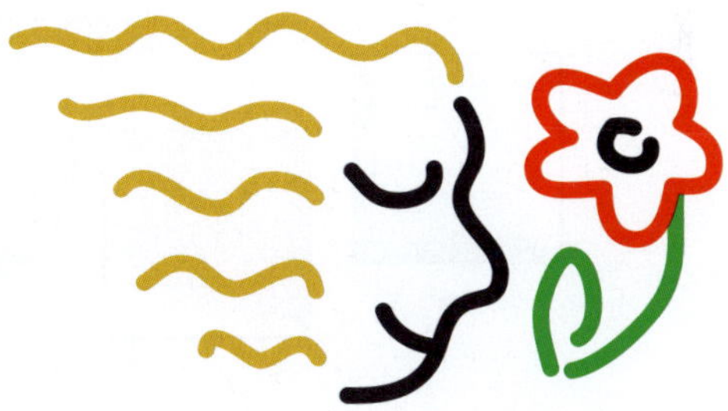

Can I do this?

Using vector-based software tools, make sure you can:

Use freehand tools

Combine basic shapes and freehand drawing

▸▸ Activity 2.12

Explore your software to find out what freehand tools you have available. How can you make use of them for The Project?

Adding effects

How can you make your drawings more realistic? This is where you can use your imagination to make use of the special effects that your software offers.

Special fills

Shapes can be filled with colours, patterns or textures. These can be used to make objects look solid or three-dimensional, or to make them stand out.

Shadows and 3D-effects

Drop shadows can be used for emphasis and to provide a 3D-effect on a flat object. You can control the properties of the shadow, such as colour, size, intensity and position.

The drop shadow added to the square makes it stand out. In the second drawing, the square has been moved and the position and size of the shadow changed to produce a more exaggerated effect.

In this sequence an inner shadow has been added to the first object. This gives an effect of transparency. The second object has an inner glow and the third an outer glow.

These objects have all been created using an inner bevel effect. The size and lighting direction has been varied and an additional outer bevel has been added to the largest hexagon. The bevel effect will make basic filled shapes look like solid objects.

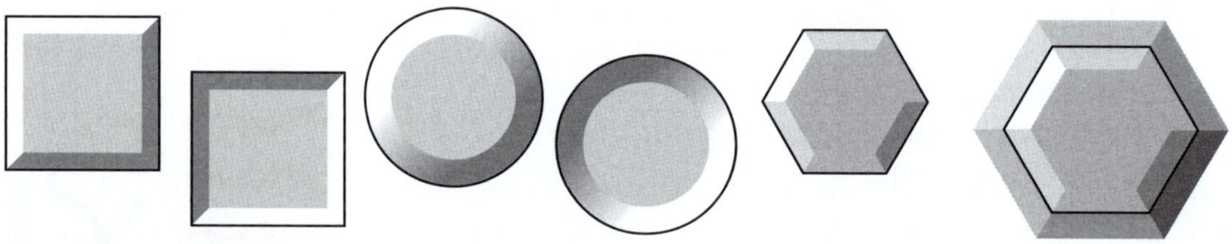

Can I do this?

Using vector-based software tools, make sure you can:

Use shadows and 3D-effects **Edit the stroke**

▸▸ Activity 2.13

Use the techniques described above to improve your workstation drawing. Colour the worktops, chairs and IT equipment in appropriate colours. Add shadows to create a 3D-effect.

Gradients

Gradients are fills with two colours. The colours are blended gradually together. The results can make a flat colour more interesting and give the impression of a 3D-effect. You can control the direction of the colours.

The drawing opposite uses a diagonal gradient for the sky and a horizontal gradient for the water.

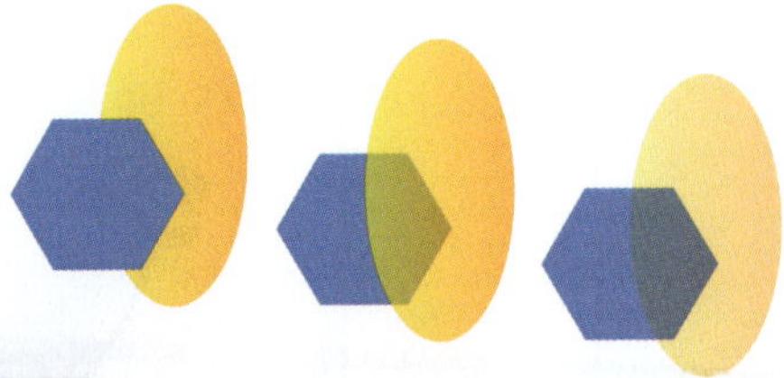

Transparency

Fills and gradients are used to create solid objects, but sometimes it may be necessary to make filled objects transparent. Your software may allow you to control the degree of transparency.

In this example the solid ellipse has been made transparent and faded into the background.

Activity 2.14

Have a go at producing your own versions of the drawings above using vector software tools.

Can I do this?

Using vector-based software tools, make sure you can:

Alter the properties of the fill

Activity 2.15

Follow the instructions below to produce a drawing of a dice. Use the tools and effects of your software to get the best results possible. Copy each drawing ready for the next step so that you can reproduce the image below.

1. **Draw a basic square with a red fill. Draw a circle with a yellow fill.**
2. **Round the corners of the square. Send the circle to the front and duplicate it.**
3. **Bevel the edges of the square and add a drop shadow.**
4. **Copy, paste and reposition the circle.**
5. **Rescale and align the circles.**
6. **Enlarge the drop shadow and add an inner shadow to the circles.**
7. **Add a graduated background and then copy, paste, rotate, resize, reposition, crop and make the dice transparent.**

Patterns

Patterns can be used as shading or to suggest the texture of materials. Your software should allow you to fill shapes and objects with pre-set patterns. Patterns also have properties such as scale and colour.

Activity 2.16

Extend your workstation drawing to include a floor area. Use a suitable pattern and colour for the flooring.

Can I do this?

Using vector-based software tools, make sure you can:

Add patterns

Layers

Layers help you to organise a drawing. By placing objects on different layers you adapt the same drawing for different purposes by turning the layers on and off. For example, you may add coloured fills and patterns on one layer for presentation purposes, or you may decide to make a layer just for the dimensions and scale. You will still be able to view the basic line drawing by turning the presentation layer off. The drawing can then be viewed without displaying any unwanted details.

Layer 1 The basic outline

Layer 2 Fills

Layer 3 Background

Can I do this?

Using vector-based software tools, make sure you can:

Use layers in vector images

▸▸ Activity 2.17

Create a copy of the vector drawing of the picture above using layers as indicated.

▸▸ Activity 2.18

Open the individual workstation drawing. Add dimensions and scale to a separate layer. Add fills and gradients to the objects in another layer. Then, in another layer, add drop shadows, or other effects, to the objects to give them depth. Experiment by turning layers on and off to create a 'working drawing' version and a 'presentation version' of the plan.

Text

Don't forget that text is also an important graphic element, not just what it says but how it looks.

Left aligned. Im do hez consenibh endit lorperciduis accum incilis od ciliqum doloboreet nummodo lestio euguero.

Right aligned. Im do hez consenibh endit lorperciduis accum incilis od ciliqum doloboreet nummodo lestio euguero.

Centred. Im do hez consenibh endit lorperciduis accum incilis od ciliqum doloboreet nummodo lestio euguero.

Fully justified. Im do hez consenibh endit lorperciduis accum incilis od ciliqum doloboreet nummodo lestio euguero.

Text effects

Size

The size of the text you use will depend on the target audience and the purpose. How far away will the audience be? Text is scalable and can be sized to meet requirements without losing quality.

Font style

Font style is a difficult choice because there are so many. Try to relate the style to your audience and purpose. For example, a simple sans serif font such as Arial is easy to read and is a good choice for forms and leaflets.

TALKING POINT 2.3

Look at each of these fonts. Are the styles associated with particular purposes? Can you describe a target audience that each font might be used for?

Graphics	Graphics	Graphics
Graphics	**GRAPHICS**	Graphics

Enhancing text with strokes and fills

As with other vector objects, the colour of the stroke can be controlled separately from the fill.

Using different coloured strokes and fills means you can reflect a colour scheme in the text, or provide a strong contrast to highlight your message.

Can I do this?

Using vector-based software tools, make sure you can:

Insert, format and edit text

Edit the stroke of text

▸▸ Activity 2.19

Experiment with designs for text you could use on the poster for THE PROJECT. Keep samples of any combinations of font, colour and design you think work well.

Gradients and patterns

Gradients can be used to enhance appearance and to direct attention towards your main message. You may need to convert your text into an object before you can add a gradient or a pattern.

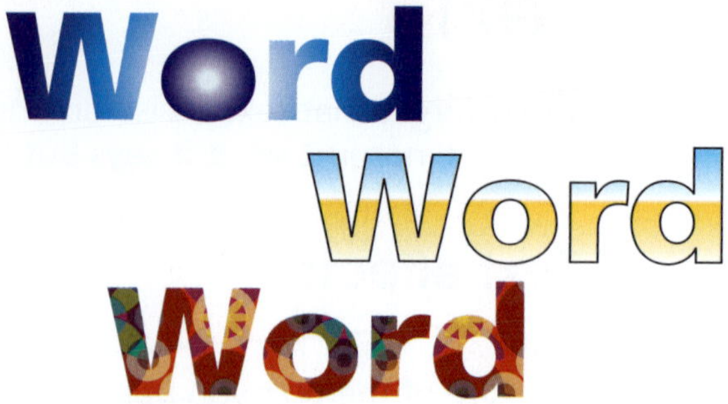

Attaching text to shapes

Text can be made to follow a shape by drawing the required shape and then attaching the text to it. In this example the text has been attached to a curved line. This approach can be developed so that the words take on the shape of the object being described.

Can I do this?

Using vector-based software tools, make sure you can:

Use text effects

Fit text to path

▸▸ Activity 2.20

Many of the products you will create for THE PROJECT will include the name of the cafe.

Experiment with fills, gradients and other text effects in your software to create a style for the Cafe 21 name. Discuss your results with others. Here are some examples that may inspire you.

TALKING POINT 2.4

Should there be a limit to the number of effects you use? How do you decide when to stop making changes?

Making use of vector graphics

Logos

Logos appear on all sorts of graphic products. They need to convey their message with clever simplicity, using few colours and a combination of text and graphics.

It is often helpful to design a logo in black and white first. That way you get a much better idea of the shape, design and readability of the logo. You also make sure that the logo will work when it needs to appear in black and white. When you add colour, stick to a few colours and make sure that they will have the desired effect.

Remember that it doesn't matter whether you like your logo. What matters is that it works for your target audience.

TALKING POINT 2.5

Good designers will keep their logo designs simple. Why do you think this is? Think of some famous logos that follow this rule. What colours do they use? What makes them so effective?

Vector graphics are good for logos: they lend themselves well to simple, clear shapes, can be resized without distortion, are easily recoloured, and their file sizes are likely to be small and manageable.

Can I do this?

Using vector-based software tools, make sure you can:

Save vector images

▸▸ Activity 2.21

Produce some ideas for a logo for Cafe 21 using vector-based software tools.

Scale drawings

Often a drawing cannot show a plan or an object at its full size because it is too big to fit on the screen or on paper. Scale drawings can be used to provide the necessary design information by reducing everything down in the same proportions. Equally, if an object is very small, the drawing can be enlarged to show detail more clearly.

Scale

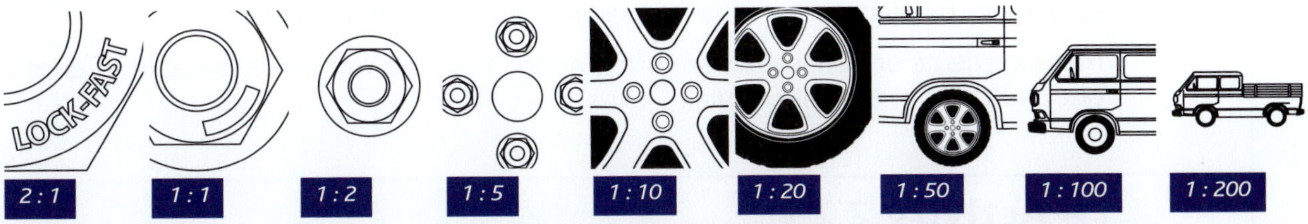

These are the scales most often used for 2D drawings, although maps need much larger scales. Compare the drawings at 1:5 and 1:50. Note that the smaller the scale the more detail you can show, but the larger the scale the more you can cover.

How do you choose the scale? As you might expect, it depends on the audience and purpose! People involved in making a product such as flat-pack furniture need drawings that are simple and easy to follow with just enough detail. People considering different design ideas need an overview of the design.

Vector-based software packages often have powerful zoom facilities. It is possible to zoom into a layout plan to add fine details.

▸▸ Activity 2.22

Pick a large object that you can easily measure, choose a suitable scale and create a scale drawing of it from above. Show the dimensions and scale on a different layer.

Now create a drawing of a wristwatch using a scale of 3:1 (not 1:3!).

Plans

Plans show what something looks like from above. They are usually drawn to scale and accuracy is very important. Imagine the consequences if the plans for Wembley Stadium were inaccurate! If an object is 900 mm square, it must be drawn to be precisely 900 mm square on the plan, or the correct measurement using an appropriate scale.

Measurements or dimensions are often added to plans. You should be able to print them out and check them with a ruler.

▸▸ Activity 2.23

Draw a plan of a household object such as a teapot, kettle or frying pan. Include dimensions and the scale on the drawing.

Elevations

Elevations are scale drawings of the front, back or sides of an object. They illustrate overall appearance and provide details that cannot be conveyed on a plan, such as heights. They are often used to present design ideas.

Main elevation

House, front elevation

Computer, rear elevation

> **Activity 2.24**
>
> **Draw a front and side elevation of the object you chose for Activity 2.23, including a scale and dimensions.**

Nets

How is a chocolate box made? What about a carrier bag? These are both 3D graphic products but they are created from 2D card or fabric. A net shows the shape of the material before it is cut out and folded to make the product.

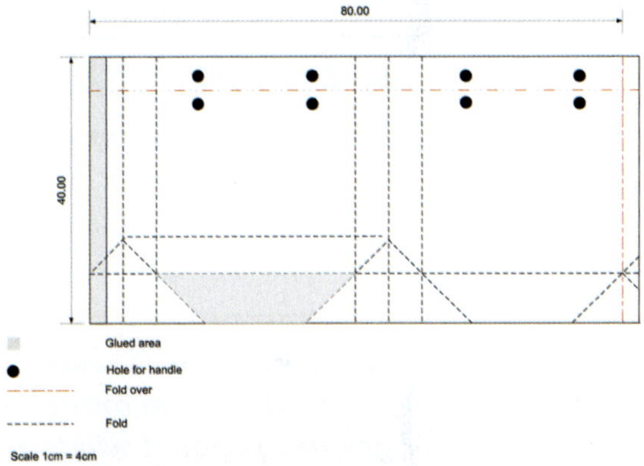

TALKING POINT 2.6

Look at the net for this Cadburys Creme Egg packaging. Can you see how it folds to make the finished box?

> **Activity 2.25**
>
> **Collect some 3D graphic products made of paper or card and take them apart to reveal their nets. Look at this example of a chocolate box.**
>
> **Choose one product and create a scale drawing of its net. Cut out the net and fold it. Is it a true representation of the original?**

Surface elements

Once you have a net for a product, you can add the surface elements you plan to include. This means positioning the graphic elements on each surface.

You can then use your 2D scale drawing to show how a finished product will look by cutting out the net and assembling the product. Take care to position your elements correctly!

▸▸ Activity 2.26

Add some surface elements to your net for the product you chose. Be careful to position each element correctly. When you fold it up, is each element the right size and the right way up?

▸▸ Activity 2.27

Sketch some designs for a gift box. Choose one of your designs and draw an accurate net for it. Add surface elements to the lid and to the sides of the box. Cut out and assemble the box. Did it turn out as you expected?

TALKING POINT 2.7

Creating a scale model of a product is just one way of showing what a finished graphic product will look like. What else could you do?

Representations

When you produce initial and detailed designs for products you will need to get feedback on your ideas. How will you show people what a finished product will look like? Try to be creative and offer your test users as much information as possible.

This T-shirt design is shown by adding the graphic elements to an existing image of a T-shirt and to a vector drawing of a T-shirt.

An alternative would be to create a transfer and iron it on to a real T-shirt, but that might be taking things too far at this stage!

Web graphics

The internet is an excellent place to see examples of vector graphics. Most web pages have vector elements such as banners and buttons. These elements are designed and combined to help create an overall product that is targeted at a specific audience.

Banners

A banner is used to grab the viewers' attention. Many banners incorporate animated text or images.

TALKING POINT 2.8

What makes a good banner? Are text effects widely used? Do you think animated banners are a good idea? How are banners related to audience and purpose?

Buttons

Buttons are used to help people find their way around and navigate between web pages. They need to be obvious, attractive and fit in with the rest of the page. Your software may offer you ready-made button designs like these. Button designs will use many of the vector techniques covered in this chapter.

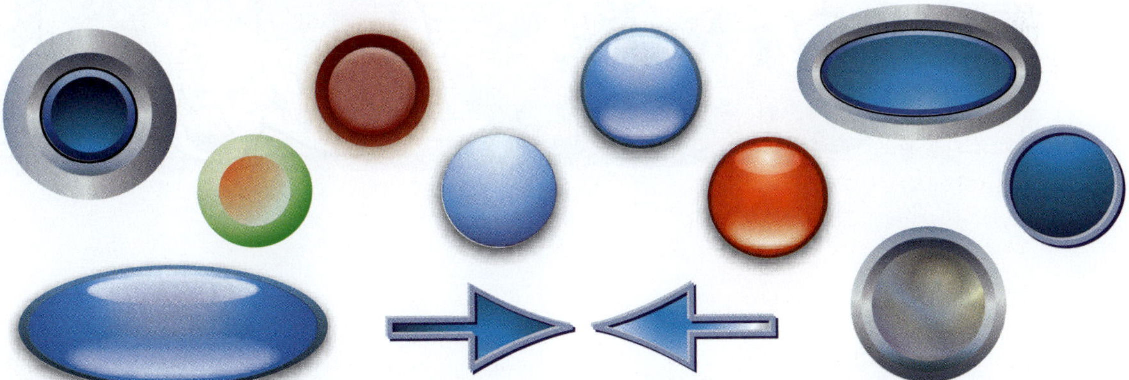

▸▸ Activity 2.28

Use your vector tools to experiment with buttons and banners that you might use on the home page for Cafe 21.

▸▸ Activity 2.29

Most web authoring software includes a library of ready-made buttons. Find out what your package offers.

Tackling THE PROJECT

P

Although you're not ready to start designing your products for THE PROJECT, you can think about how you will make use of vector tools to produce elements for them.

Have another look at the requirements for THE PROJECT.

Exploring ideas should be your focus at this stage. You have already made a start on this for the logo, the banner and buttons for the home page, and text for the poster and cafe name. Where else might you use vector graphics?

Take this opportunity to practise your vector graphics skills. Experiment with the tools your software provides, trying out as many different techniques as you can. Don't throw anything away – your first ideas might be your best.

You don't have to do this work in isolation. Share your ideas with others in your group and help each other to develop a good toolkit.

If you see a graphic element you like in the world around you, see whether you can use your vector skills to duplicate it.

3 Working with bitmap graphics

Look at the images in glossy magazines and on CD covers. Most of these are bitmaps based on digital photographs.

A bitmap can show the fine detail of an object close up or accurately represent the colours and shadings of a landscape. It can be used to show something to its best advantage by editing to cover up the defects.

A bitmap consists of hundreds, or thousands, of tiny dots. Every dot can be a different colour and can be edited separately. This gives you limitless opportunities to change fine details. You can touch up photographs to give someone perfect teeth or change a sky from day to night.

There can be a price to pay for all this detail – the higher the quality, the bigger the file. Don't get carried away creating a fantastic bitmap only to find you don't have room for it or that everyone gets bored waiting for it to download!

In this chapter you will learn how to create and edit bitmap graphics by:

- ***adjusting canvas size and colour***
- ***manipulating pixels***
- ***applying special effects and filters***
- ***adding text***
- ***using layers and combining bitmaps***
- ***optimising quality and file size***

3 Bitmap graphics

Whenever you take a photograph or scan an image you are producing a bitmap. A bitmap image is made up of tiny dots, called pixels, stored in a grid.

The pixels are usually too small for the human eye to see, but you can enlarge a bitmap graphic to show individual pixels. These pixels can then be edited individually, making very fine changes possible.

Activity 3.1

Find your home area on Google Maps. Select the satellite view. Zoom in and out a few times. Now do the same with the map view of the same area. What are the main differences between the map and satellite views? What type of graphic is each one? Why are both provided?

What are bitmaps good for?

Bitmap images are used for a variety of purposes, for example:

- to give information or to show what something looks like
- to record important or interesting events
- to advertise products or services
- on packaging
- as decoration on objects such as buildings or clothing.

TALKING POINT 3.1

Look at the list of uses of bitmap graphics above. Can you think of an example of a bitmap being used in each of these ways? What is the audience and purpose in each case?

Using a canvas

When you want to create or edit a bitmap, you need to work on a canvas. When you open a new document in your bitmap graphics software you should see something like this. The menus allow you to set options for the canvas.

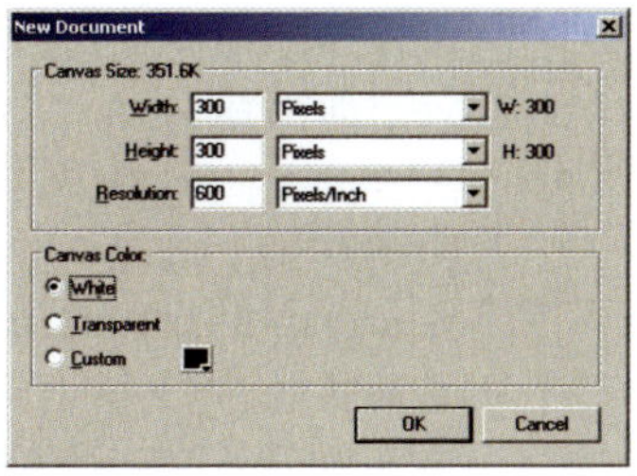

First you have to decide how big you want the canvas to be. You can set the measurement in inches, centimetres or pixels.

Next you must choose the canvas colour. The standard options are white, transparent and custom. The option you choose will depend on what you plan to do on the canvas.

If you want to use a colour other than white for the background, click on the colour swatch and select a colour. The transparent option is useful when you are combining parts of images or if you want to transfer an image onto an existing background, for example if you are creating an image to add to a web page.

Editing the canvas

You can change the size and properties of the canvas after you have begun working on a graphic.

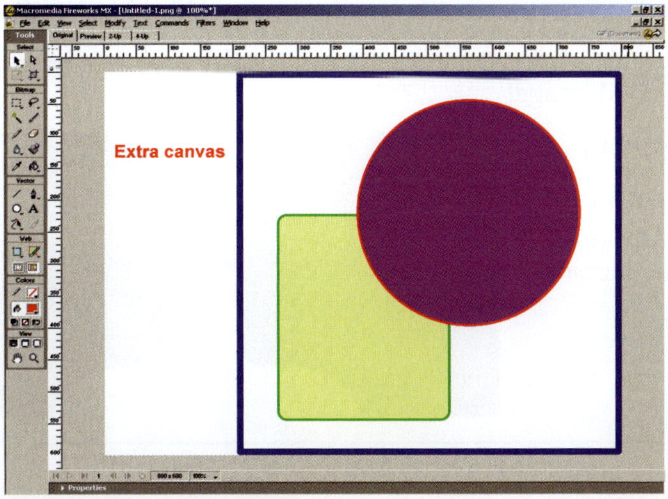

If you increase the canvas size it will appear in the selected colour, or be transparent if you have chosen that option. By default, the extra canvas will be added all around the image.

Here, extra canvas has been added to the left of the image. You can decrease the canvas size to crop an image.

Can I do this?

Using bitmap-based software tools, make sure you can:

Adjust canvas size for screen and print

Activity 3.2

Open a new document in your bitmap graphics software and choose the canvas size and colour you want. Add this image to the canvas and practise changing the canvas properties to see how the image is affected.

3

Manipulating bitmaps

Many of the tools available in bitmap software are similar to those you have used for vector graphics.

Resizing

Resizing a bitmap allows you to make it bigger or smaller. The size is changed but the content remains the same. The bitmap below has been resized.

If you make a bitmap bigger, you make each individual pixel bigger. At some point the picture will start to look blurry and, even worse, you will be able to see individual pixels. Unlike vector graphics, there is a limit to how much you can resize a bitmap.

You must be careful to keep the proportions correct when you resize a bitmap or you will end up with a squashed or stretched image!

Copying and flipping

You can copy and paste a bitmap in the same way that you copy and paste text. You can create a mirror image by flipping a copy of the image.

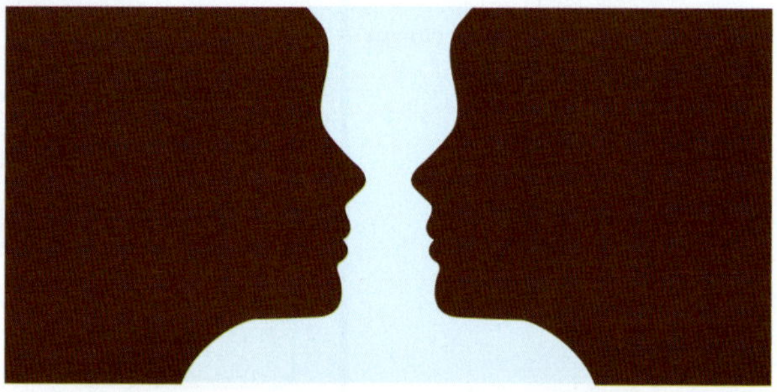

Can I do this?

Using bitmap-based software tools, make sure you can:

Resize bitmaps

Cut and move bitmaps

Copy and flip bitmaps

Activity 3.3

Open this image in your bitmap graphics software. Save it to your user area. Resize the image so that the dimensions are doubled then save it again with a different filename. Compare the file sizes.

How big can you make it before the image gets blurry?

Use the image to practise copying and flipping images.

Selecting parts of an image

You may want to add an effect to just part of a bitmap. For example, you might want to darken the sky in a photograph, move an object such as a car or simply delete something. You can do this by selecting the area you want to change.

A marquee tool allows you to drag over an area of an image and select it. The tower in this photograph has been selected using a marquee tool.

Alternatively you can use the lasso tool, which allows you to select an irregular shape.

If you have drawn the image yourself, you can use the pointer tool to select part of the image.

Can I do this?

Using bitmap-based software tools, make sure you can:

Select an area of a bitmap

Activity 3.4

Open this bitmap file and practise using the marquee tool to select parts of the image. Try to select the body of the car by using the lasso tool.

Cropping

If you want to use only part of an image you would use the crop tool. In this photograph the area containing the seagulls was selected and then the image was cropped.

Skewing and distorting

You can change the shape of a bitmap by using skew or distort. This image of a football has been skewed.

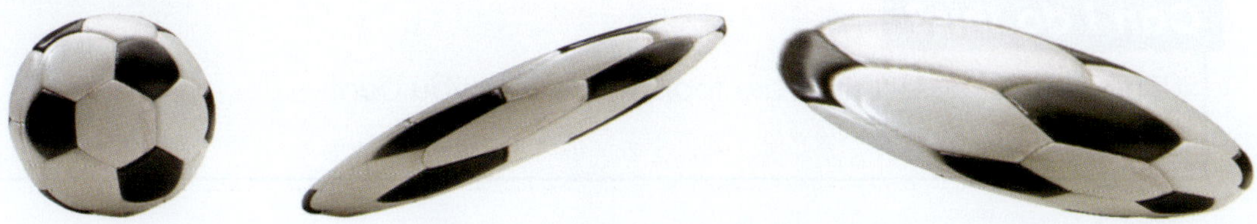

Can I do this?

Using bitmap-based software tools, make sure you can:

Crop a bitmap

Skew and distort a bitmap

Activity 3.5

This file contains the bitmap image of the football shown on the previous page. Try skewing it to make it look like a rugby ball.

TALKING POINT 3.2

Look at some of the photographs in your favourite magazines. Do you think any of the images were edited before they were published? If so, why do you think this was done? What tools do you think were used? Is there anything wrong with manipulating photographs?

Selecting pixels

You have already seen how to select whole areas of a bitmap, but often you need to change smaller areas.

Zoom in

Your bitmap graphics software will allow you to zoom in to enlarge an area of a bitmap until you can see the individual pixels.

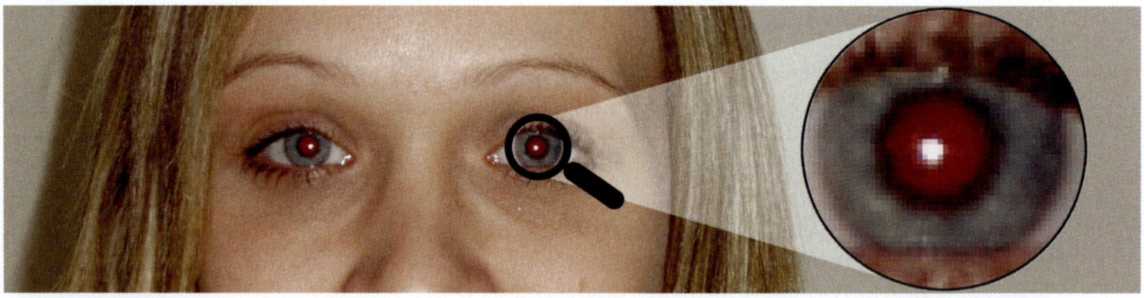

Magic wand

Most graphics packages have a tool like the magic wand, which allows you to select pixels of a particular colour. In this image the white pixels have been selected.

Can I do this?

Using bitmap-based software tools, make sure you can:

Select pixels

Editing pixels

Colour

You can change the colour of selected pixels using the palette or by copying a colour from elsewhere in the graphic.

This poster shows how much an image can be changed just by altering the colour on all or part of it. You can change the colour of an image in lots of different ways.

By selecting pixels you can change the colour of very small areas.

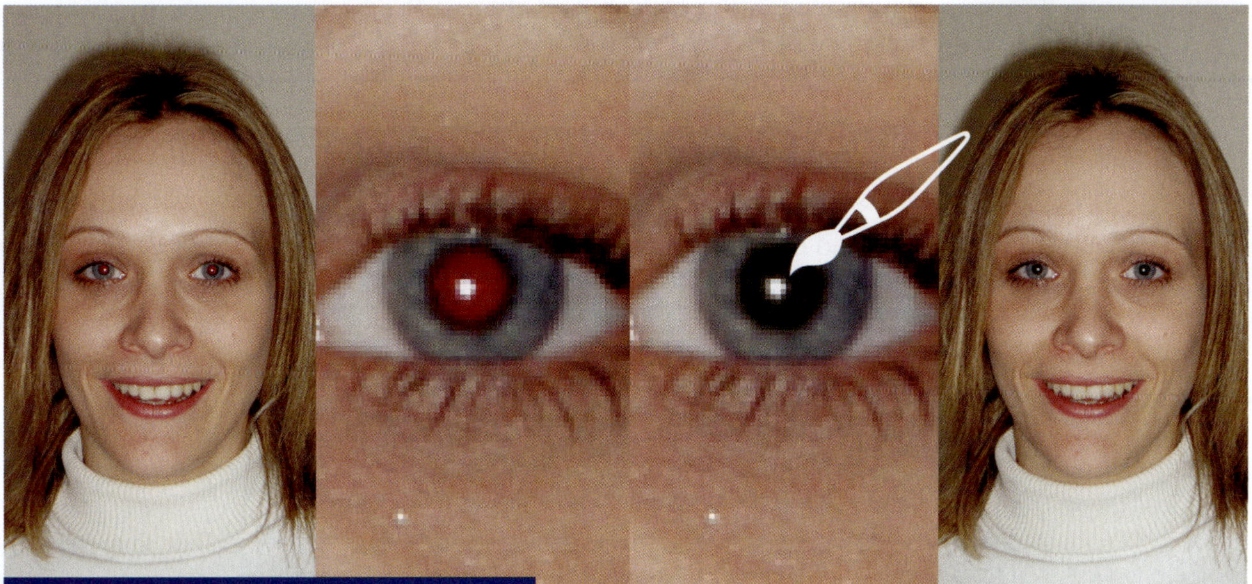

Try correcting the red eye in this photo yourself

If you zoom in until you can see individual pixels, you can then use the brush tool to paint each pixel the required colour. The image on the right is a tiny area of the flowers photo, zoomed to 800%. To change larger areas, you can simply paint straight onto the image using the brush tool.

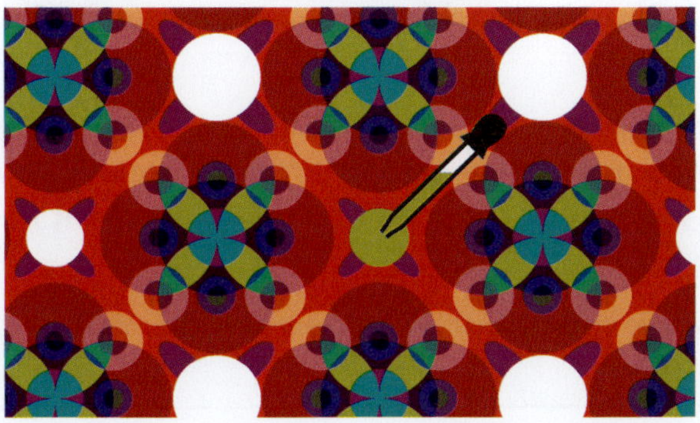

The eyedropper tool allows you to sample an area of colour in a photograph and drop it into the fill colour so that you can get a perfect match for any colour in your image.

Here, the white circle was filled with a colour selected from another area of the image using the eyedropper tool.

Can I do this?

Using bitmap-based software tools, make sure you can:

Change the colour of pixels

▸▸ Activity 3.6

Open this file and select the roof of the car, using the magic wand if necessary. Change the roof to plain white using the palette. Choose a colour you like from somewhere else in the picture and change the body of the car to this by using the magic wand and eyedropper tools.

You can change the overall effect of the colour in a photograph, for example to make a photograph taken on a dull day look as though the sun was shining. Most bitmap-based software allows you to change the hue, saturation and brightness of colour.

The hue command is used to flatten out colour. Look at this picture of water lilies – the hue has been increased and the contrast between the pink and green reduced.

In this version the saturation and brightness have been increased with the result that the colours are much brighter and the contrast is greater.

Another way to change colour is to increase the strength of one colour in an image. Below are four versions of the same image. The original picture is on the left.

If you want to change just one area of an image, you will need to copy the selected pixels to a new layer.

▸▸ Activity 3.7

Take a digital photograph of someone you know and make four copies of the image. Adjust the colours in the photograph, applying different options to each copy. Resize the images so that you can fit them all on an A4 document and print them.

Repeat the process, but now change the colour of just part of the image, for example the subject's hair or clothing.

Cloning

Sometimes you have a photograph that would be ideal for your purpose if you could just alter a small part of it. Cloning allows you to replace areas with pixels from somewhere else in the photo. You place the cursor on the area you want to copy and paint over the area you want to remove. In this image the bee has been cloned.

Eraser

The eraser tool allows you to 'rub out' pixels just like an ordinary eraser. This is useful if you have painted colour in the wrong place and want to remove it. Some of the black pixels in the second version of this image have been rubbed out, revealing the canvas underneath. You can change the size and shape of the eraser to make it easier to rub out different shaped areas.

Can I do this?

Using bitmap-based software tools, make sure you can:

Clone and erase pixels

▸▸ Activity 3.8

Open this photograph of Venice in your bitmap graphics software. The crane spoils the image. Remove it by using the cloning tool. Try removing the boat in the foreground to make the canal look less busy. Use the crop tool to select the gondolas, enlarge them, and make a new image. Save the edited image in your user area as you will need it again.

Adding effects

Dodge and burn

The dodge and burn tools allow you to lighten or darken an image. Here the dodge tool was used to make this night scene look like dawn.

Can I do this?

Using bitmap-based software tools, make sure you can:

Apply special effects to bitmaps

Activity 3.9

Open this file, which contains the original of the photograph shown above. Use dodge and burn to create the same effects. Experiment with using these techniques on other bitmaps you have saved.

Filters

Most bitmap-based software packages allow you to apply a special visual effect called a filter. You can use this technique to make a photograph look like a watercolour or an oil painting. You can also add texture, blur or sharpen an image, or change the lighting effect.

A simple filter, such as mosaic, will keep the original colours but change the appearance of the image. You can change the image even more by adding several filters. You can add a filter to a whole image or select part of an image using the tools we looked at earlier in this chapter.

Neon glow changes the colour of the flower and fades the background, and poster edges sharpens the edges of this image

Activity 3.10

Use the original image of the flower shown above to create similar effects to those shown by applying filters. Experiment with other effects.

Activity 3.11

Look at this example of an oil painting. Your bitmap-based software can even help you achieve effects like this! Open your edited image of Venice and use filters to turn it into a picture in this style.

Activity 3.12

This file contains a number of bitmap graphics. Use them to practise all your bitmap software skills.

Text in bitmaps

Look at any magazine, newspaper, poster, leaflet or product packaging and you will see combinations of text and images. For example, this poster is designed to attract the attention of students. They are likely to be familiar with baked beans, but the blue beans will make them look more carefully and read the text.

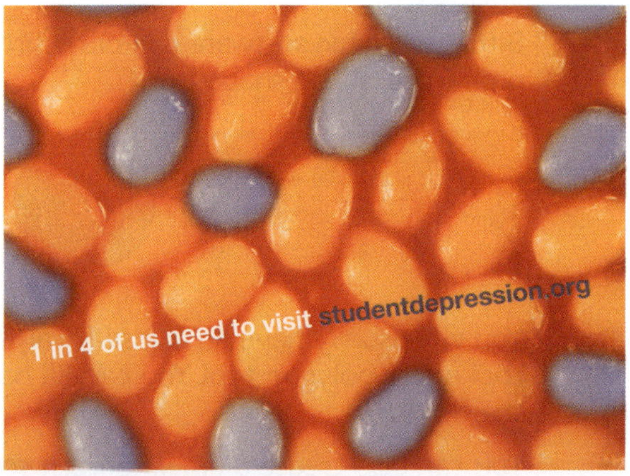

▸▸ Activity 3.13

Look through your favourite magazines to find examples of text being used with bitmaps in interesting and creative ways. Keep your examples as a source of ideas for THE PROJECT.

The text tool allows you to add text to a bitmap image. Click on the text tool, then click on your image and type the required text.

You can use effects to make the text reflect a theme from the product so that it appeals to the target audience. In this example the font, colour and point size have been changed using the text menu. You can make text more interesting by changing its shape or orientation.

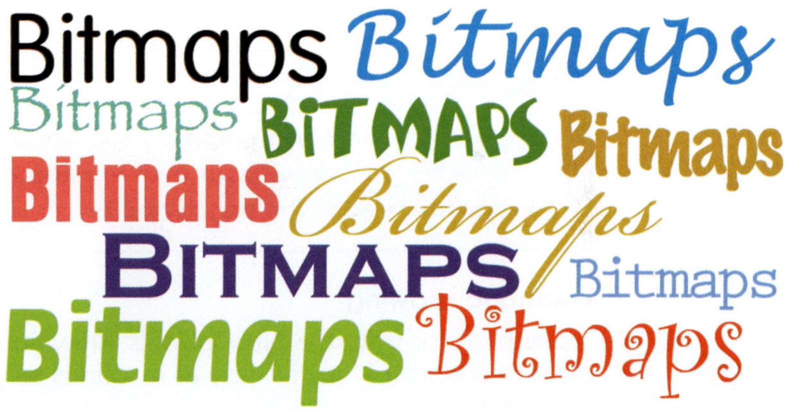

Can I do this?

Using bitmap-based software tools, make sure you can:

Insert, format and edit text

Change colour, font and font size

▸▸ Activity 3.14

Experiment with designs for text you could use on the products for THE PROJECT. Keep samples of any combinations of font, colour and design you think work well.

Shapes and freehand

Shapes

Bitmap graphic software can draw simple shapes for you. You can set the size and properties of the shapes.

You will usually have an ellipse (oval) tool, a rectangle tool and a polygon tool. You can fill basic shapes using the fill tool.

You can also create a drawing from scratch using the shape, brush and pencil tools in your bitmap software. You can change the colour of the fill, brush and pencil strokes by selecting a colour from the palette.

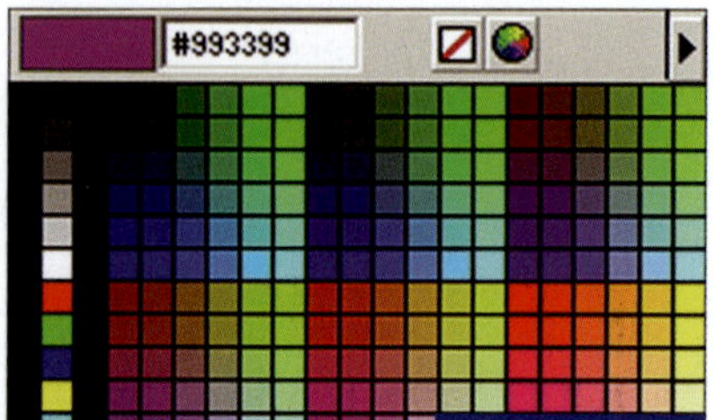

The palette

Can I do this?

Using bitmap-based software tools, make sure you can:

Draw and paint bitmaps

▸▸ Activity 3.15

Explore your bitmap graphic software and find out which basic shapes it will create for you. Draw your own version of the collection of shapes shown above. Experiment with the pencil and brush tools as well as other properties.

Freehand drawing

As with vector software, bitmap tools allow you to draw freehand. It is not as easy as it sounds so you need to practise!

Can I do this?

Using bitmap-based software tools, make sure you can:

Create freehand drawings

▸▸ Activity 3.16

Use freehand tools to add features to these mugshots, such as a moustache, glasses, a fringe or freckles.

Grouping

You will find that you can't move or resize an image made up of different objects unless you first group the objects to form one image. You can ungroup it again if you want to edit or delete part of the image.

Textures, patterns and fills

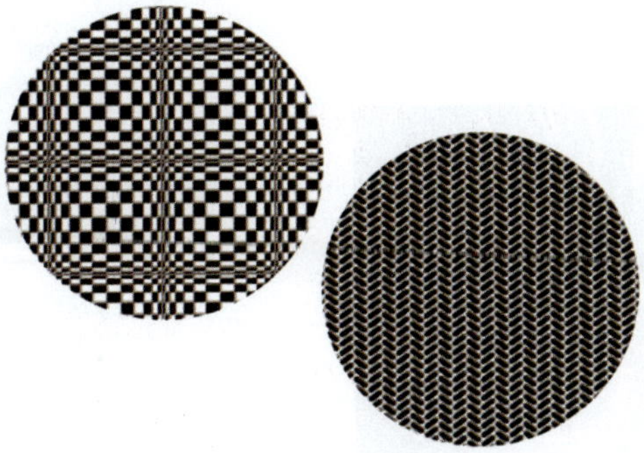

Special effects such as textures, patterns and fills can be used to enhance your bitmaps. These effects can be used to make a bitmap more realistic or simply to add a decorative effect. The two circles on the left contain a simple fill effect.

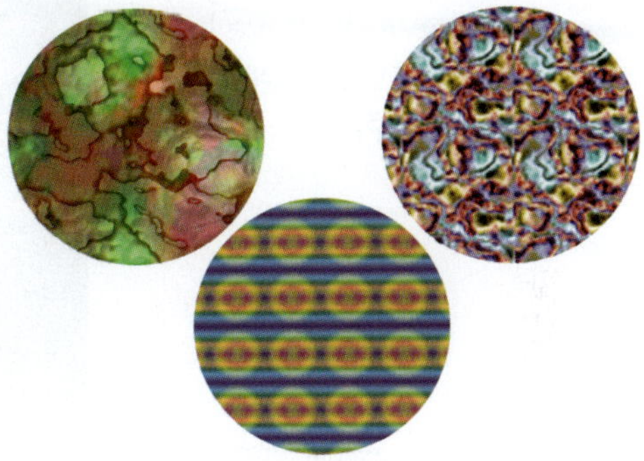

The three circles on the right contain different textures with added colour.

The square on the left was filled with an effect called bars, the middle image shows the options available to edit the effect, and the image on the right shows the edited effect.

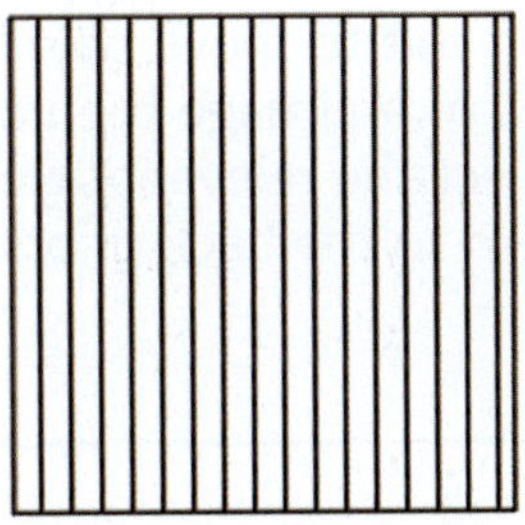

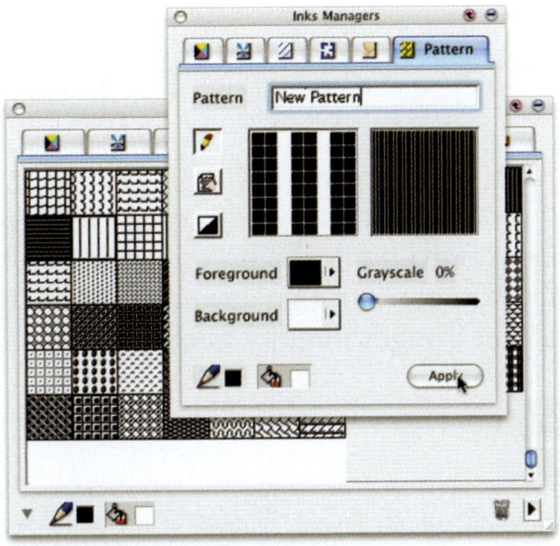

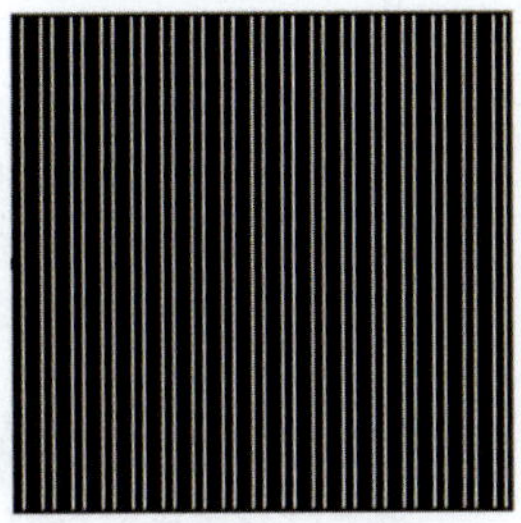

▸▸ Activity 3.17

Create a wallpaper design for a child's bedroom. Use your bitmap graphics software to draw some shapes and experiment with different fills and textures. Some packages will even allow you to use a piece of clipart or a photograph as a fill. Compare the effects with the rest of your group.

Keep a record of the tools you used to create any really good effects as you may want to use them for THE PROJECT.

Combining bitmaps

You might want to take parts of several different bitmaps and put them together. For example, you could combine photographs you have taken with images from secondary sources, drawings or text.

This Coldplay poster combines a large photograph of the band with text and a graphic from the album cover. This technique is often used in advertising.

You can use similar techniques to produce images of your own. For example, images of fireworks have been added to this original photograph.

TALKING POINT 3.3

Which of the tools you have looked at so far could have been used to add the fireworks to the original photograph? If you are not sure, try doing something similar yourself.

Layers

Using layers will help you to combine and edit images. It is difficult to move objects around if they are all on the same layer. You can select an area of an image then copy and paste the selected pixels onto a new layer. You will have to select the relevant layer to edit the image stored on it. You can 'arrange' layers by sending them to the back or bringing them to the front so that images overlay each other.

Can I do this?

Using bitmap-based software tools, make sure you can:

Use layers in bitmaps

Combine bitmaps in a composite image

▸▸ Activity 3.18

Use these two bitmaps to produce a new image with the butterfly perched on the flower. Use a layer to help you position the butterfly. Use another layer to annotate your image to explain what you have done.

Quality and file size

Colour systems

Imagine ordering a T-shirt from a website only to find that the colour is a different shade from the picture in the catalogue.

The colours must be accurate to avoid complaints so the retailer should have used a more extensive colour range to produce the web graphics.

The T-shirt the customer receives ...

... doesn't look the same as it does in the web catalogue!

TALKING POINT 3.4

Look around you – how many colours can you see? Don't forget that as far as a computer is concerned, every shade counts as a different colour and it has a unique code.

256 colours might be enough for a simple image where different shades are not important, but when accuracy counts you need to use the full range. How many is enough? If you decide that 256 colours aren't enough then the next step up is 16.8 million, and that should be plenty! However, there is a price to pay in terms of the amount of storage space needed.

TALKING POINT 3.5

Look at the difference that the number of colours makes to the sea scene and its file size. Can you think of situations where you might choose each of these and when you should avoid using them? What factors do you need to take into account when deciding how many colours to use?

Greyscale is another colour system you will find useful – don't assume that full colour is always best. It provides 256 shades of grey from pure black to pure white and is used for monochrome images, such as 'black and white' photographs.

Colour palettes

A colour palette restricts the colours that can be used in an image. Your software will allow you to choose from a number of different palettes. The web-safe palette is particularly useful as it prevents you from using colours that may not work in some browsers or on mobile phones and PDAs, which can have limited graphics capability. You can customise a palette to suit your needs – for example, by including many shades of the same colour or colours that are part of a corporate identity.

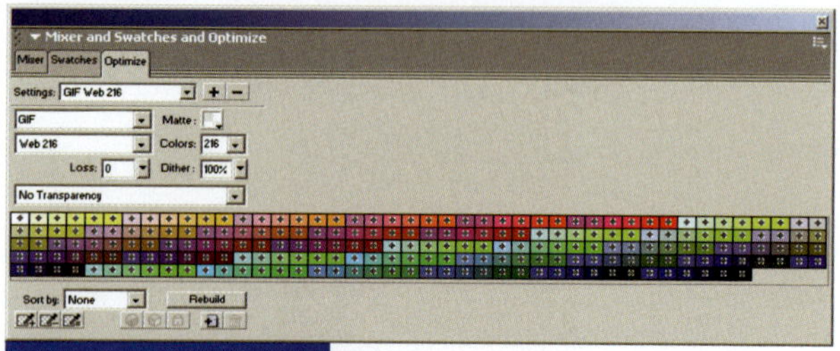

A web-safe palette

Can I do this?

Using bitmap-based software tools, make sure you can:

Use levels and curves

Convert images to greyscale

Choose and customise colour palettes

Adjust colour balance

Activity 3.19

Use these images to experiment with colour systems, colour palettes and colour balance.

Resolution

Colour isn't the only thing that affects the quality of a bitmap. Quality also depends on an image's resolution – the number of pixels (or dots) per inch (dpi). You need to use a high resolution to produce a high-quality image, but again there will be a price to pay in terms of file size.

You must remember that resizing a bitmap does not alter its file size unless you also change the resolution. For example, if you make a bitmap bigger you will lose quality but the file size will stay the same.

TALKING POINT 3.6

Why does the file size stay the same if you resize a bitmap image to make it smaller or bigger?

Activity 3.20

Open this bitmap file. Experiment with the resolution and resave it to see what happens to the file size.

File formats

When you are saving an image you must choose an appropriate file format. You need to know what you are going to use the image for and where you are going to use it. For example, is it going to be published in a magazine, printed on a poster or used on the web?

There are a number of different bitmap graphic types. The format you use will depend on what you plan to use the bitmap for.

JPEG

Bitmap images need to be high quality if they are to be used for print-based graphic products, such as glossy magazines or posters. The JPEG format allows a vast number of different colours. Digital cameras produce JPEG images by default.

However, JPEGs can take up a lot of storage space. For example, an A4 image when printed at a resolution of 300dpi will be about 25MB. For this reason, they should be used with care in screen-based products and avoided on web pages where download times need to be kept to a minimum.

Open this bitmap file and investigate its size

GIF and PNG

GIF and PNG files are relatively small, but the images are limited to a maximum of 256 colours. One advantage of these formats is that you can set the transparency so that colours on another layer show through. GIFs and PNGs are ideal for web graphics where file size and download speed are important.

Can I do this?

Using bitmap-based software tools, make sure you can:

Save bitmaps in appropriate formats

Tackling **The Project**

P

You can continue to explore ideas for **The Project** and improve your bitmap skills at the same time.

Start collecting digital photographs that might be useful for your products. You might not be able to take pictures at a real internet cafe, but there are plenty of useful shots to be found without leaving your centre. People working at computers, eating their lunch, mugs of coffee ... the possibilities are all around you!

Don't forget to ask permission before taking people's photographs, even if you know them.

Experiment with bitmap tools, trying out as many different techniques as you can. Don't throw anything away – your first ideas might be your best.

Try out different file formats and resolutions, but don't forget to save a copy of the original first as you might want to return to it later.

Share your ideas with others in your group and help each other to develop a good toolkit. If you see an element you like in the world around you, see whether you can use your bitmap skills to duplicate it.

4 Who, why, where, what, how?

A graphic product relies on visual communication to get its message across. The choice of graphic elements will be crucial to its success, so how do you decide what to use? The more you know about the audience and purpose, the more likely you are to get it right. You will be working to a brief and you must make sure that you understand the requirements.

Other people have good ideas and you can make use of these to help you be creative. You should look for sources of inspiration in similar products and in the world around you.

Before you spend too much time on the details, make sure that you are on the right track by producing initial designs and asking other people what they think of them. You need to present your design ideas clearly and explain your thinking to test users. It is the audience's opinion that really counts.

It is not always easy to work out how a design has come about. You need to keep a record of how you progress from initial ideas right through to the final product, and you should start now.

In this chapter you will learn how to produce initial designs for a graphic product by investigating:

- ***who the target audience is***
- ***why the product is needed***
- ***where it will be viewed***
- ***what medium must be used***
- ***what must go in it***
- ***sources of inspiration***

Who is it for?

What is the point in producing a graphic product if the audience doesn't notice it, doesn't like it or is even turned off by it? The more you can find out about your audience, the more likely you are to produce products that work for them.

The target audience

The target audience is the group of people that you want to reach and affect in some way. It could be an individual person, a small group (such as a local football club) or a broad section of society (such as football fans).

TALKING POINT 4.1

Look at these three book covers. The titles have been removed. Can you describe the three target audiences? What titles would you give these books?

When a band releases a new CD, their aim is to sell it. They have a target audience but they are in a very competitive market place. They don't just need to attract attention; they need to make sure that the people who stop and look are those most likely to buy their CD.

CD covers are now also viewed in online stores, such as Amazon

TALKING POINT 4.2

Look at some covers for CDs on Amazon. Do they all attract attention? Do some stand out less than others? Does this matter? Think about who the target audience might be for each CD. Will the target audience be attracted by the cover or will they be looking for it anyway?

TALKING POINT 4.3

These two graphic products have a similar purpose but are intended for different audiences. What are the main differences and similarities between them? Who is the intended audience for each?

▸▸ Activity 4.1

Use a mind map or a table to list all the products in The Project. Add as much detail as you can about the audience for each product. The more you find out now, the easier it will be to produce good designs later.

Why is it needed?

You've been asked to produce a graphic product, but what's the point of it? Why is a graphic product needed at all? As with any other publication or product you need to be clear about the purpose. Why are graphic elements needed and what must they achieve? The product may be a website that needs to inform, an advert that needs to persuade or a digital poster designed simply to attract attention. These are just a few examples – you must establish exactly what the purpose is before you start on the design of any graphic product.

TALKING POINT 4.4

What other purposes can you think of for graphic products? What does the purpose tell you about the graphic elements you may need?

Do you want to persuade people?

Some campaigns aim to persuade people to change their actions or opinions. Graphic images are used to strengthen the main message.

TALKING POINT 4.5

How does this picture of a harpoon gun make you feel? What other feelings or emotions can images prompt? How could these feelings help a particular campaign?

Activity 4.2

Choose a children's charity. Find a selection of images that could be used to persuade people to donate money to this charity.

Do you want to attract attention?

If you need to grab the attention of passers-by, you will need a graphic product with impact – something that stands out, with bright colours, strong contrast and bold text.

In this World War I recruitment poster the emphasis on 'YOU' attracts attention and the pointing figure is difficult to ignore. Can you ignore someone in a crowd who appears to be pointing at you?

It would also be difficult to walk past this young man without stopping to read his message – whatever that may be!

Activity 4.3

Find some examples of graphic products designed to attract attention. Who is the audience and where would they be found? How has this influenced the design of the graphic? Does the choice of elements work?

Do you want to communicate without words?

Sometimes it is important that there is no misunderstanding.

TALKING POINT 4.6

Pictograms are simple symbols that avoid using text. They overcome language difficulties and can be useful in places such as international airports. Can you think of other uses and examples of pictograms?

Do you want to impress someone?

Your purpose may be to impress, perhaps to present a new product or business. If this is the case then your graphic elements will need to be high quality. No matter how good a product is, poor-quality graphics are likely to drive customers away.

TALKING POINT 4.7

What impression do the elements used in each of these adverts give?

Do you need to be accurate and precise?

If someone is going to use your drawing to make something, it must be correct and accurate. All manufactured products start off as a set of graphic instructions. If these instructions are not accurate, the product will not work as intended.

TALKING POINT 4.8

What happens if graphics are not fit for purpose? What problems might occur as a result of any misunderstanding? Could inaccuracies in some drawings have serious consequences?

▸▸ Activity 4.4

Look at these examples of graphic products and identify the target audience and purpose for each. Are they effective?

▸▸ Activity 4.5

Add notes about purpose to your mind map or table of products for The Project.

Where will it be viewed?

The location of a graphic product will influence its design.

Brief encounter

Many graphic products are viewed in passing. These products need to attract attention and convey a message quickly and effectively. Even then, the time available for viewing varies. People on a bus pass by a billboard very quickly, so an advert here would need to get its message across in just a few seconds. Delivery vans are also used to promote businesses and products as they move around an area.

In contrast, people on a tube escalator are a captive audience. They are moving along slowly and can even be 'told a story' through a series of advertisements. However, each poster needs to convey a short, sharp message, whether it stands alone or is part of a series.

Some locations provide unique opportunities. Times Square in New York is full of digital posters and illuminated graphics which compete with each other for attention. Many cities in the UK have similar graphic products on display, even if they are not quite so spectacular!

Some products need to have an immediate impact even when the audience is static, for example a TV commercial. In contrast, a poster on the wall of a doctor's waiting room can be more detailed because the audience is closer and has more time to look at it and read it.

Close encounter

Some products can contain more detail and convey a stronger message provided that they first capture and hold the audience's attention. TV commercials, web adverts and websites, shop displays and exhibition stands all aim to attract people's attention, enticing them to look closer.

Other graphic products are designed for detailed viewing at home or in a workshop, such as diagrams for self-assembly furniture or car maintenance.

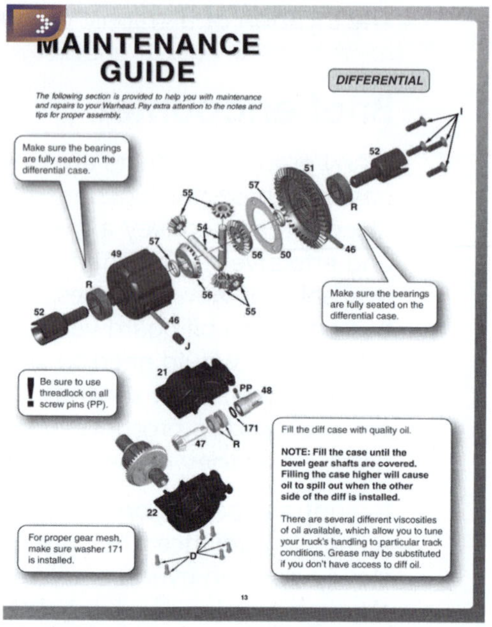

Marketing and promotion are becoming more and more important in a competitive world, whether it's a chocolate wrapper, a charity wristband or a free gift. With these graphic products, the audience has time to take in more information or to absorb a message.

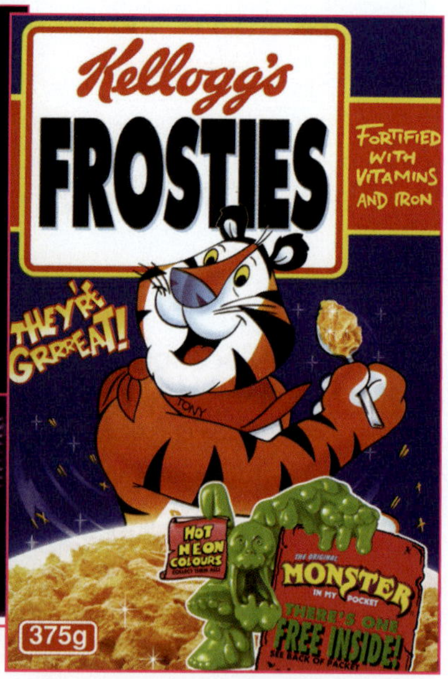

TALKING POINT 4.9

Pick three different locations, for example a high street, supermarket and leisure centre. What graphic products can you find in each location? How has the location influenced the design of the products?

▸▸ Activity 4.6

Add notes to your mind map or table of products for THE PROJECT to show what you know about the intended location of each product.

What must go in it?

Once you know the audience and purpose of a product and its intended location, you need to think about what must go in it.

What does the brief say?

You will be working to a brief that specifies what must be included in a product. For example, the brief might specify the dimensions, materials, colours, medium and/or wording to be used. There might also be technical requirements, such as file size and type.

▸▸ Activity 4.7

THE PROJECT is a brief for a number of graphic products. Remember, if it's in the brief, it's non-negotiable!

Go through the whole brief now and make sure that you are clear about the requirements for each product. Add the details to your mind map or table.

What else would you expect to see?

There will often be standard components that should be included even though they are not specified in the brief. For example, a magazine cover would need an issue number, a date and a title. A net for a chocolate box or carrier bag needs a scale and dimensions.

▸▸ Activity 4.8

For each product in THE PROJECT, identify everything else you think must go into it. Add the details to your mind map or table.

How do you make your mark?

However detailed the brief, there is always room for you to be creative. When designing your products you will need to meet the requirements of the brief, but you will also have lots of different ideas about how you will make the products work.

Look at this brief for the design of a book cover. Below are some samples produced by different designers – different front covers for the book all produced to the same brief. Even though each designer was working to the same brief and knew what else usually appears on a book cover they each came up with something completely different.

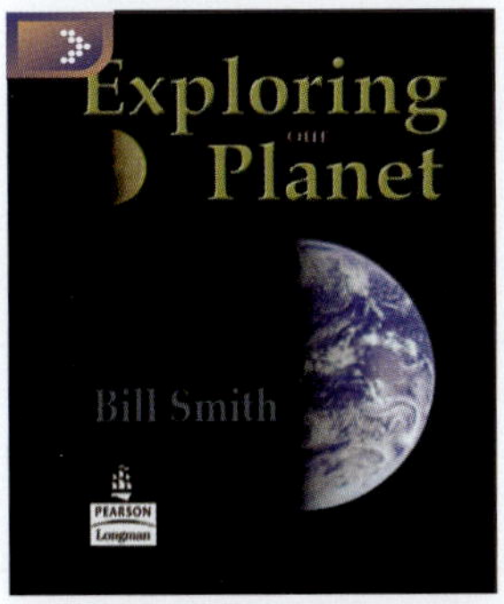

TALKING POINT 4.10

Discuss the competition entries shown above. Each designer followed the brief. What do you think was specified? What tools have been used? Has each designer been creative?

How will you go about it?

Spending time at the beginning of a project investigating who, why, where and what always pays off. Once you know what is needed, you can start to design a graphic product that will do the job well.

Sources of inspiration

Where will your first ideas come from? You have lots of experience of this already from your work on other DiDA units. You should know about gathering stimulus materials – looking at other people's ideas and using them to develop your own.

Other people's ideas

Has anybody else ever completed a similar project? The answer is probably 'yes' – hundreds of times. There is nothing wrong with looking at other people's work to get ideas. You are not going to copy them directly, you just want to see what has worked well in the past. Designers of graphic products have always been inspired in this way.

You might be flicking through a magazine and think 'That view would be a great background for my poster' or 'If I could enlarge that section of the photograph I could use it in the centre of my logo'.

Alternatively, you might be inspired by a favourite book or album cover. In 1967 Peter Blake and Jan Haworth designed the cover for the Beatles album Sgt. Pepper's Lonely Hearts Club Band. The design is a fantasy audience made of a collage of life-size photographs and waxwork images of famous people.

TALKING POINT 4.11

Could you use this album cover as inspiration and create a collage for any of the products in **The Project**? *Do you think it would work? What graphics software would you use to produce this?*

Other peoples' sketches, drawings and paintings will stimulate your ideas. Even sketches showing ideas that were rejected could be interesting – you may decide that these could be adapted to suit your purpose. Diagrams, maps and plans can offer ideas for layout and presentation. They can also illustrate various approaches to using colour and text. Did you know that the designer of the London Underground map was inspired by a circuit diagram? The list of potential sources is never-ending!

The world around you

The world is full of colours, textures and shapes and this is what graphic products are all about. Of course, the great thing about using nature for your ideas is that you never have to ask permission!

This student has taken a photograph of daisies in a field and then manipulated it to make a background for a product. She has also adapted the idea for a related product. This technique is simple, but effective.

⏩ Activity 4.9

Look outside and count the colours you can see. Look for interesting shapes – a branch of a tree, a rock or stone, for example. What about textures? How could you imitate what you see in nature in your designs?

TALKING POINT 4.12

These websites both include elements inspired by nature. Can you think of other examples of graphic products where something in nature has influenced the design in some way?

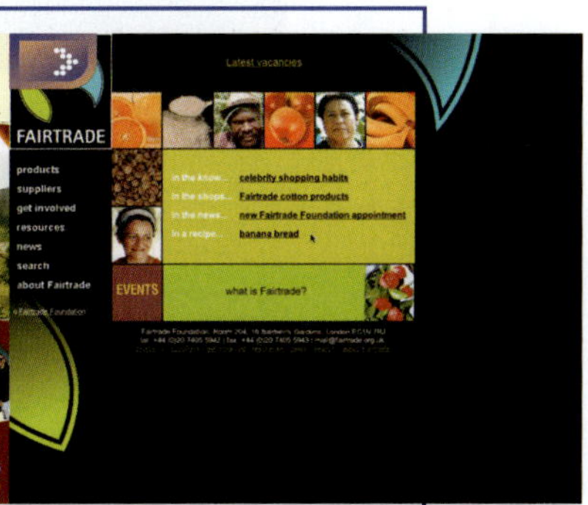

⏩ Activity 4.10

You need to get some ideas for THE PROJECT. Look for stimulus materials in magazines and newspapers, or on the internet. Take a camera to your local high street or shopping centre and take photographs of anything that inspires you. Keep a record of where you find the material.

⏩ Activity 4.11

Some of the graphic products in THE PROJECT, such as the web page banner, the poster and the sign, require you to add text. Look out for striking typefaces or fonts. If you see an interesting font and colour combination, keep it or take a photograph of it. Save these examples for future reference.

Initial designs

Once you've done your research and are feeling inspired, you may be tempted to get your hands on the software and rush into creating the final products. But of course you won't because you know by now that spending time on design will pay off later!

You will also know that design is an ongoing process rather than a one-off task. Initial designs allow you to gather your thoughts and check that you are on track before you go any further. They also allow you to experiment with different approaches and find out what people like best.

The sum of many parts

The final product will only work if every aspect of it is right. You need to think about the elements that you need as well as the product itself. For example, if you are producing a chocolate box, you need to sketch a net for the packaging, but you also need to consider all the surface elements that you want to put on it.

Visual links

Imagine if the McDonald's 'M' was red on signs, blue on kid's packs and green on adverts. What if they used a different font on each product too?

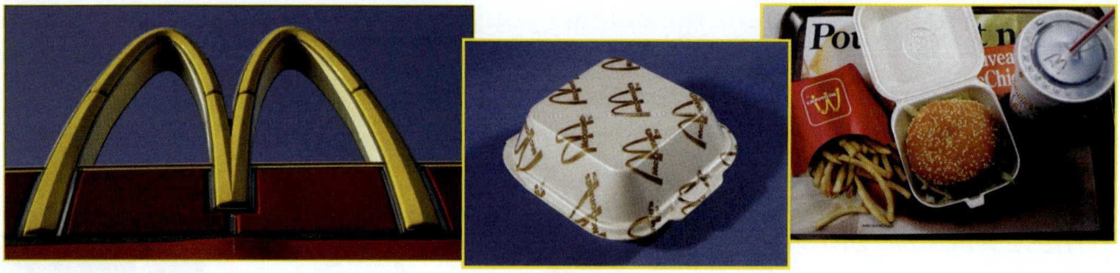

Products that are related need to look as if they belong together. This can be achieved by using visual links such as common elements, colours, fonts or shapes in your designs. Consistent positioning of elements, such as the logo or main headings, can also help.

TALKING POINT 4.13

These books are part of the same series. Identify all the visual links between them. Do the links work? What else would you do?

TALKING POINT 4.14

All the products in **The Project** *are for Cafe 21 so you will need to use visual links. How can this be achieved?*

Activity 4.12

Take another look at your ideas for the Cafe 21 logo. Will they work on all the different media, in different sizes? Does the logo need to have just a single colour on any of them?

What might initial designs look like?

Initial designs are for you and whoever you want to get feedback from. How you produce them is up to you. What matters is that you can organise your thoughts and communicate your ideas to others.

Hand-drawn sketches

Good old-fashioned pen and paper can be a good place to start! You can scribble away without worrying about accuracy or detail. You could get your ideas down on paper by doing some sketches: here is a sketch for the design of the home page of a website. You can show your sketches to other people and ask for their opinions.

Computer sketches

For those of you who cannot bear to be parted from your computer, you can make use of your graphics software to produce initial sketches.

Mock-ups

It is often difficult for people to visualise how your designs will look as a finished product, especially if the graphic product is three-dimensional. You might need to produce a rough mock-up, for example by folding your sketch of a net to make a box or gift bag.

Alternatively, you could try using a similar product to create your mock-up – for example, you could take a mug and stick your sketched design on it.

Sample features

You could show people other products using similar features such as pattern, shape, colour or medium. Then describe to them how you will use these features: 'I'm using the outline of the flower on this T-shirt in the centre of my mug design' or 'I want to create the same effect as this concrete path for my background'.

Activity 4.13

Produce initial designs for the Cafe 21 kids' pack, home page and mug. Use your research and the stimulus material you have gathered to give you ideas. Experiment with different methods of producing the designs, such as a mock-up for the kids' pack and a sketch for the home page.

Getting feedback on initial designs

There is still so much to do. Your ideas are sketchy, literally, so why take up people's time getting feedback now?

TALKING POINT 4.15

Why should you get feedback on initial designs? Does it matter who you ask?

Asking the right people

It's no good asking wrinklies like us what we think of your design for a kids' pack! You need to ask someone who is either a member of the target audience or someone who can remember being that age.

If, however, you are designing a T-shirt for an adult, our feedback might be worth considering. There is no point in asking the opinion of a classmate, but you could ask your teacher or parents.

Ask people who can make sound judgements about what you are doing. If you can't get to members of your target audience, find people who are close to it in age or interests.

Ask as many people as you can and compare what they say.

▸▸ Activity 4.14

Who will you ask to act as test users for your initial designs? Decide who you will ask for each product, making sure that they will be able to give useful feedback.

Asking the right questions

If you show a sketch to someone and just ask what they think, they might say, 'Yeah, it's really cool', or 'Gosh, that must have taken you ages', or perhaps, 'It's ok, but I like mine better'.

TALKING POINT 4.16

What do you think of this feedback? Is it helpful? What could have been done to get more useful feedback?

You will only get useful feedback if you ask the right questions. Ask your test users to focus on particular features, by asking questions like: 'Do you like the colour of ...?' or 'Is the logo big enough?'

Keeping a record

Unless you have the memory of an elephant, you will need to find a way of recording the feedback you receive at each stage of the process. If you have used a questionnaire, you can add the responses to it. Alternatively, you could ask test users to annotate your designs with their comments. Any method will do as long as it works for you.

Activity 4.15

Decide what you want to ask each test user for THE PROJECT. Try different methods, including a questionnaire and an interview. Get feedback on your initial designs and keep a record of what the test users say. If you find you have not asked the right people, find some more.

Deciding what needs to be done

The idea of feedback is to check that you are on track and to firm up your ideas. But you don't have to do everything your test users say! Go through all the feedback and use it to make decisions. You will be able to reject some of your ideas and alternatives so that you can move on to more detailed designs.

Activity 4.16

Go through the feedback you have collected on your initial designs and refine your ideas. Reject features that are clearly not going to work. You will know when you have done enough because you will be confident that you can now produce detailed designs for each product.

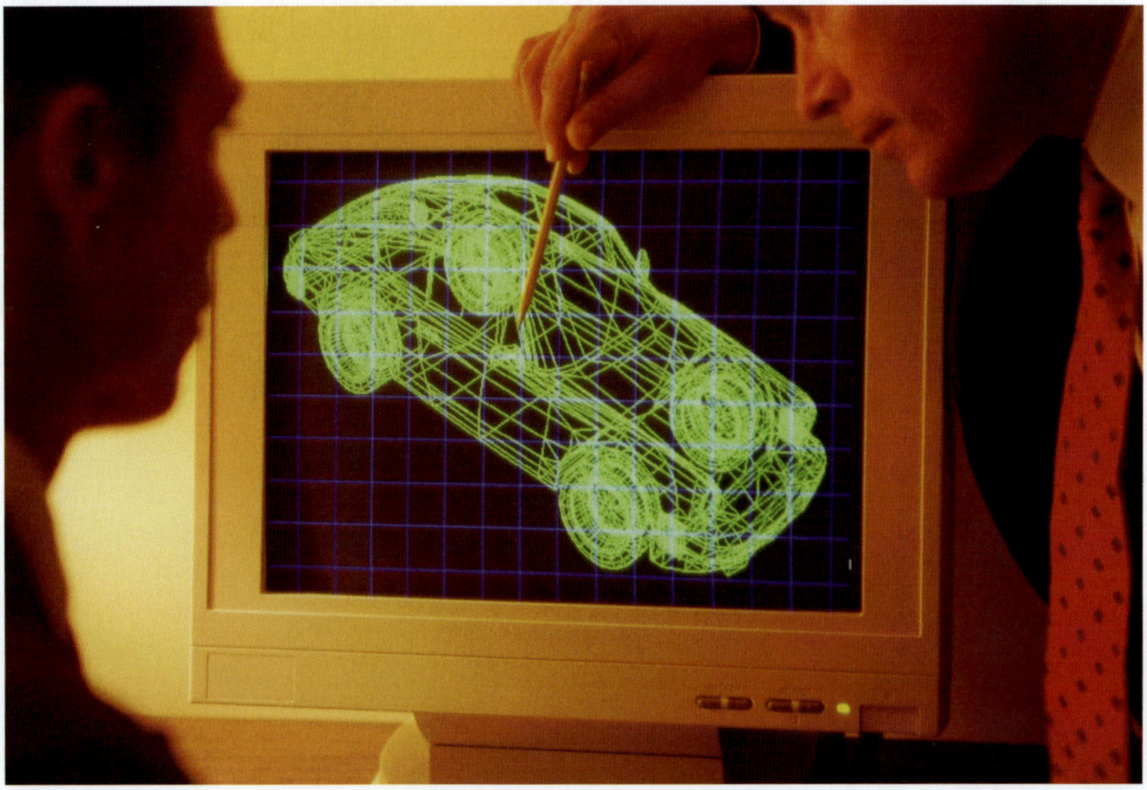

Tackling THE PROJECT

P

By now you should be clear about the audience and purpose of each of the products, where they will be used and what content is required.

You should have found some sources of inspiration to give you ideas for the products.

You have made a start on firming up those ideas by producing initial designs for the logo and three of the products: the kids' box, the home page and the mug. If you chose your test users carefully you will have received useful feedback and refined your designs.

How did you present your designs to others? Did you make good use of bitmap and vector tools to present them?

Working on the other products

Go through the same process now for the other two products: the poster and the sign.

Use your ideas and sources of inspiration to produce initial designs and get some feedback on them.

Making use of feedback

Was the feedback you received really useful? Did you ask the right people? If not, find someone else before you move on to the next stage of the process. Get it right and you will be able to ask the same people again when you produce detailed designs and the products themselves.

Keeping records

Make sure you keep a record of your initial ideas. You should also save the feedback you receive and notes on how you used it.

5 Developing graphic products

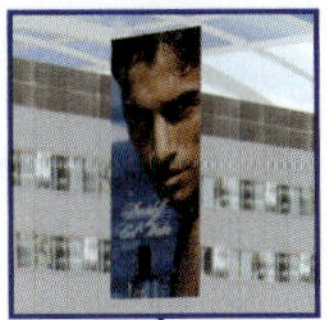

Once you have firmed up your initial design ideas for a graphic product, the next stage is to produce detailed designs. These should give an accurate impression of what you are planning to do and explain your design decisions.

When you have detailed designs in place, it's time to get to grips with the practical aspects of gathering all the elements you need. You should be able to get some from secondary sources, but you will also need to apply your graphics skills to produce elements of your own.

You will use graphics tools to build prototype products. Remember to make good use of your designs. As a general rule, if it's not in the design, it shouldn't be in the product. However, if your prototypes are not right, you will need to revisit your designs.

The other key success factor is the quality of your testing. You must choose the right people to give you feedback. It is also important to allow enough time for them to do the job properly and for you to repeat the production cycle as many times as necessary to get the product right.

This might sound like a lengthy process, but when you do it for real you will find that one stage runs seamlessly into the next. This is your chance to enjoy yourself and be creative!

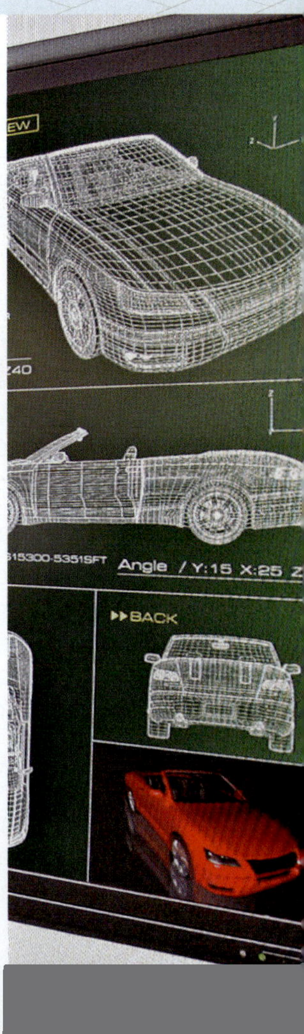

In this chapter you will learn how to develop effective graphic products by:

- ***communicating detailed design decisions and making use of feedback***
- ***gathering graphic elements***
- ***combining elements and making them work together***
- ***producing prototypes and representations***

Detailed designs

Imagine showing your final product to someone who gave you feedback on your initial design only to hear: 'But that doesn't look anything like you said it would!' or 'That's not what I thought you meant.' They may not like the colour or the images used or the layout in the final product.

If you have made good use of feedback on your initial design you should have a much clearer idea of what you are going to do, but do you really know exactly what is required? If not, how can you be sure that your product will work for the audience? You need to work up your initial design by adding detail to every aspect, both individual elements and the product as a whole.

Although this might seem like a long and painful process, it really does pay off in the end! There is great satisfaction in building a product that meets most, if not all, of the requirements first time round.

There are a number of things you need to consider when working on final designs.

Medium and dimensions

The chosen medium for your final product will have a major impact on your design. There is no point designing a leaflet with hundreds of shades and colours if your printer cannot reproduce them.

Make sure you know enough about the medium. Will it be screen, paper, fabric or some other material? What colours are possible? What is the maximum resolution?

The dimensions of the final product will also influence your design – if you design an A4 poster without realising that it will be printed on A5 paper, the results could be disastrous. If you design a net for packaging, you need to make sure that it is the right size for the contents.

TALKING POINT 5.1

*What do you know about the medium for each of the products in **THE PROJECT**? How will this information affect your designs?*

Colour scheme and background

Colour can completely change the impact of a product. Some colours are associated with particular topics or themes. Have you chosen colours that reflect the purpose of your product? Does the brief specify particular colours?

Are you using colour as a visual link between products? Will the colours work on the chosen medium? Do they work well together? Is text easy to read? Have you chosen colours that suit the purpose rather than colours you like?

The Tomato Zone uses red throughout to relect its topic

Visual links with other products

If you are producing a series of related products, it's not just colour that creates visual links between them. You will need to design common elements so that they work on different media and for products with different audiences and purposes.

Visual hierarchy

Every graphic product has some elements that are more important than others. How do you make sure that the audience notices these first?

TALKING POINT 5.2

Look at this classic poster design. What stands out most? Why? What techniques have been used to make this happen?

Making some elements of a graphic product stand out more than others is called visual hierarchy. It can be achieved using size, weight, colour or positioning.

Activity 5.1

Identify all the elements in the Great Escape film poster. List them in order of visual hierarchy – from those that stand out the most to those that have the least impact. How has this hierarchy been achieved? Do you think the designer has got it right?

You need to decide the order of visual hierarchy for the elements in a product and reflect this in your design. How will you make the most important elements stand out?

Size and proportions

The easiest way to make an element stand out is to make it bigger. One of the reasons the film title in the Great Escape poster stands out is because the font size is bigger than the rest of the text. However, making an element small so that the audience has to look closely can sometimes achieve the same effect.

Resizing elements isn't always the answer. You need to make sure that the overall composition of the design still works. Remember that some elements will lose quality if you resize them.

It can sometimes be effective to change the proportions of elements to make them stand out, for example by stretching the mouth or ears on a caricature.

Weight

Elements can be given more emphasis by increasing their weight. For example, you can make a section of text bolder, thicken the border around an image or increase the brightness or tone of an image.

Contrast

Use of contrast often stops a product being dull and boring. High contrast combinations, such as light on dark or dark on light, make elements stand out. By using different degrees of contrast you can create a clear visual hierarchy.

Positioning

When working with graphic elements you can move them around individually and place them wherever you like. This is one of the most important aspects of the design process. How do you make the right decisions about where to position elements? It is really important to try things out and get feedback on what works best.

You can draw attention to an element through its positioning. In this book, the chapter title is carefully placed at the top of each right hand page. It is not in a special font, it is not very big and it is simply black on white, but it can be easily spotted by the reader because of its position.

The way in which you position elements in relation to each other is crucial. Good positioning establishes the visual hierarchy and gets the message across. Poor positioning can be distracting, confusing and sometimes completely disastrous.

If you layer elements, you need to be particularly careful that the right things stand out and that important information is not covered up. Equally, don't be tempted to fill up all the space.

TALKING POINT 5.3

Look at the top half of the Great Escape film poster. The title, barbed wire and background image are three elements that have been layered. Why have the elements been layered in this way? Are all three layers necessary? How has the positioning of the characters been used to draw the eye from the title to the names of the actors?

TALKING POINT 5.4

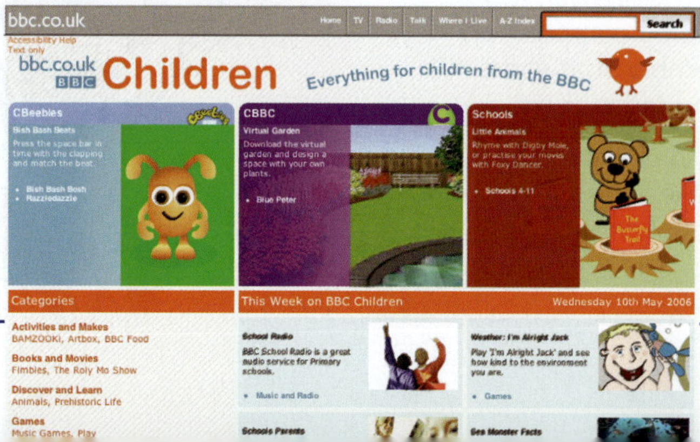

Discuss the composition of the home page for the children's section of the BBC website. What techniques are used to establish a visual hierarchy? Are they effective?

Communicating design decisions

You will only get useful feedback on your designs if the way you present them gives a clear idea of the final product. The way you do this will depend on the type of product and what you think your test users will find most helpful. Your final design must be detailed enough to give an accurate impression of what your products will look like. You should also explain your design decisions with comments such as: 'this represents …', 'I chose this because …' and 'I've placed this element here because …'.

Scale drawings

These can be drawn by hand or using ICT tools. They must be accurately drawn to scale and show where elements are to be positioned. Use text boxes or comments to add details such as what font, point size, colour and texture you will use. Don't forget to explain your design as well.

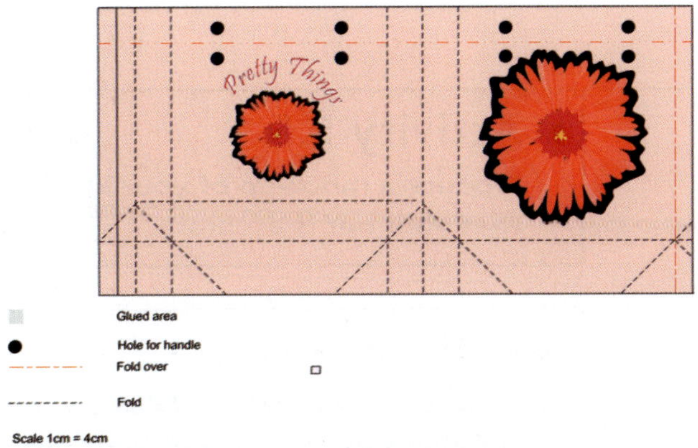

⏩ Activity 5.2

Produce a scale drawing of your design for the kids' pack. Illustrate the size and position of the various elements, including the text. Annotate your drawing carefully to explain your design decisions.

⏩ Activity 5.3

Produce a detailed design for the Cafe 21 poster. Explain your design decisions, including information about visual hierarchy. Ask someone else to describe what your poster will look like. Have you given them enough information?

Storyboards

Detailed storyboards should be used for screen-based products and must include information about multimedia assets, such as animation and sound. Again, it is important to use annotation to explain your decisions.

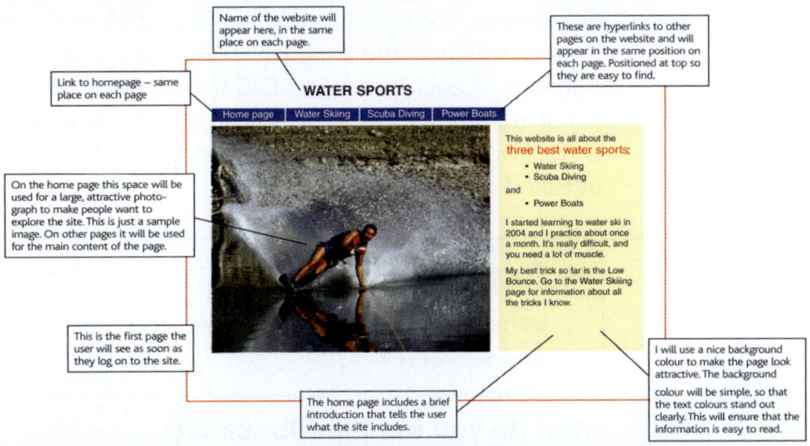

⏩ Activity 5.4

Produce a storyboard for the Cafe 21 home page. Annotate it to explain your design decisions.

Mock-ups

You may have produced a rough mock-up at the initial design stage, but your aim now is to give a more accurate impression of the finished product. If you make a model it should be carefully scaled – and that includes the design of each surface element.

▸▸ Activity 5.5

Produce a mock-up of your kids' pack to show what it will look like. Make sure that your net is accurate.

▸▸ Activity 5.6

Complete your detailed designs for the other products in The Project. Choose suitable ways to present your designs so that your test users can see exactly what you intend to produce.

Getting feedback on detailed designs

Testing it yourself

You will need to get feedback from others, but you can save time by eliminating obvious problems first. For a start, you should make sure the design meets the requirements of the brief.

Who else will test your designs?

The best people are probably those who gave you feedback on your initial designs, if you chose wisely. Decide whether you did choose the right people. If they were not members of the target audience, did they fully understand the audience and purpose of each product? Did they take time to give you constructive feedback? If the answer to any of these questions is no, find some more suitable people before you test your detailed designs.

▸▸ Activity 5.7

Who are your test users for your designs for The Project? Do you need anyone else?

What do you want feedback on?

What do you want each test user to look at? You might ask one person to test a particular aspect of a product, such as the colour scheme or the choice of images. Another test user might be asked to comment on the whole product – will it do the job, does it meet the requirements of the brief? You must make it clear to each test user what you want them to do and keep a record of their feedback.

You could help your test users by asking them questions or by creating a simple questionnaire like this one for a T-shirt design.

	Question	Comments
1	What is your first impression of my T-shirt design?	
2	What do you think of the image on the front?	
3	Is the size of the image right? Is it in a good position?	
4	Will the colours used for the graphics work on different colour T-shirts?	
5	Is it obvious what the image represents?	
6	Can you see a visual link between the T-shirt and the other products?	

Activity 5.8

Create a short questionnaire to give to the test users for your kids' pack design. Think carefully about what you want them to comment on.

Ask your test users to complete your questionnaire. Make changes to your design, taking full account of the feedback. Ask the same people to comment on the new version.

Making use of feedback

As with initial designs, there is little point in getting feedback if you don't make use of it. As well as keeping a record of what your test users say, you also need to note down what action you took as a result. You will need to show some evidence of how you developed your ideas from initial designs through to the final products.

Activity 5.9

Ask your test users for feedback on the rest of your product designs. Make changes where necessary. Ask the same people to comment on revised versions.

5

Gathering elements

Your designs will include a variety of graphic elements, such as text, photographs, symbols, maps, cartoons and computer drawings. It is now time to gather them all together. Which ones have you got already? Where are you going to get the rest from?

Using secondary sources

The internet is a good place to look for graphic elements. If you find an image on the internet, remember to use 'Save Picture As...'. This will remove the hyperlink and save the image so that you can reuse it whenever you like.

If you use paper-based sources, make sure you scan elements at an appropriate resolution.

Sometimes you might want to adapt an element from a secondary source to create something new.

TALKING POINT 5.5

What are the advantages and disadvantages of using secondary sources for your graphic elements?

▸▸ Activity 5.10

Use your detailed designs to produce a list of elements needed for THE PROJECT. Identify those that you expect to be vector, bitmap or a combination of both. Which do you think you will get from secondary sources?

Copyright

You could find an ideal image on the internet, but then discover it is copyright protected. You would be breaking the law if you just went ahead and used it. You cannot simply copy and paste any image you want, and you often have to pay to use secondary sources. You must comply with copyright law when creating your graphic products.

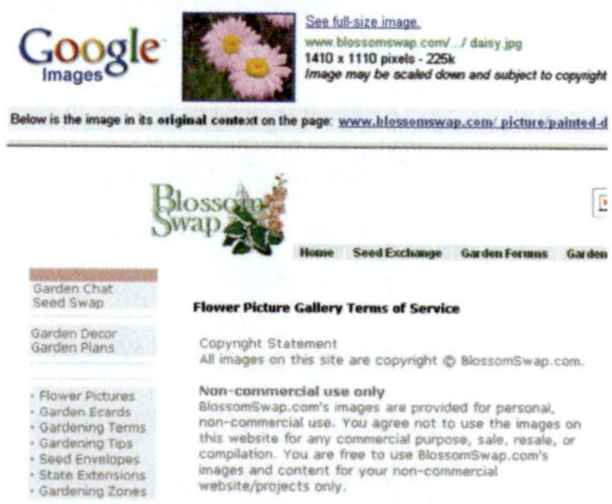

In general, material on the internet is copyright protected, although there are some sites that are 'copyright free'. You will need to check and comply with any stated terms of use, which are often found via a link from the site's home page.

Play safe and use only copyright-free materials when you can, even if you intend to adapt them to create new elements.

▸▸ Activity 5.11

Use secondary sources to gather elements for your products for THE PROJECT. Look at this list of websites that offer some copyright-free images – use these if possible or search for other similar sites. Take careful note of the terms and conditions that apply to the use of these images.

Cataloguing and recording sources

Cataloguing is a way of organising and storing elements as you gather them so that you will not waste time searching for what you want later. Use sensible file names and a logical storage structure.

Image databases

You might be able to use a database to store images in categories. You can set up your own categories and sub-categories and use the search facility when you need to find particular images. The software supplied with your digital camera might include an image database.

> ### ⏩ Activity 5.12
> **Create a suitable storage system for the elements you need for The Project. Move the elements you have already gathered into it.**

Recording sources

You need to keep a careful record of all the elements you use so that you can acknowledge your sources in your eportfolio. You could use an elements table like this one.

Elements Table, Project 203

Image (file name)	Primary/ secondary source	Bitmap/ vector/ combination	Description	Source details	Where used	Permission
skboard_005 .jpg	S	Bitmap	Boy skate-boarding	morguefile .com	T-shirt	n/a

> ### ⏩ Activity 5.13
> **Create an elements table for The Project. Add details of all the elements you have gathered so far.**

Using primary sources

There will be some elements that you definitely want to create yourself. These could include photographs, sketches and drawings, or even a new typeface.

Using elements from primary sources has several advantages:

- you are in full control
- the content and appearance of the element can be exactly as you want
- there are no concerns about copyright.

You might want to design your own letters to use on products

TALKING POINT 5.6

What are the disadvantages of using primary sources for your graphic elements?

Producing original elements

You have both bitmap and vector tools to choose from. Don't be afraid to use both if this will produce the best results. Try to be creative and think outside the box!

You might want to use traditional materials, such as crayons or oil paints, as a starting point and then digitise the results so that you can develop them further using ICT tools.

You can save time and create visual links by repurposing your own elements. This means adapting them to suit different products or purposes. For example, a multicolour logo could be repurposed to work on a single colour product such as a wristband or a medal. A photograph on a website could be cropped to produce an image link.

If you have a number of elements to create, in what order should you tackle them? If you are going out with a camera, you can save time if you take photographs for different products at the same time. Some will depend on others being created first. You can't repurpose something that doesn't exist!

Creating your logo first means you can use it on other products

Can I do this?

Using artwork and imaging software, make sure you can:

Use a digital camera **Use a scanner**

▸▸ Activity 5.14

List the elements you need to create yourself in order of priority. Make a start on producing them. The more you do now, the sooner you will be able start building your products.

Prototyping and testing

Once you have completed your detailed designs and gathered the elements you need, you can start building your prototypes. Don't expect this to be an easy process – allow plenty of time for it. Your aim must be to produce graphic products that are fit for the audience and purpose.

Don't expect to get it right at the first attempt. You must test your prototypes yourself and get feedback from others. If they are not right, you must revisit your designs.

Note people's reactions when they look at your prototypes. Where appropriate, display them in context, for example a poster could be displayed on a wall. Although you may have good feedback from test users on a detailed design, you may find that their feedback on the prototype is completely different.

TALKING POINT 5.7

Why do people sometimes react differently to prototypes than they did when they saw the detailed designs?

The production cycle

At this stage it is worth reviewing the production cycle.

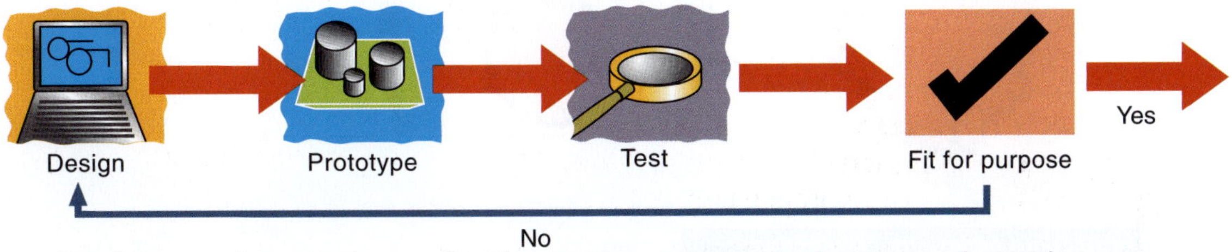

As this diagram shows, you need to keep repeating the production cycle until you are satisfied that a product is as good as it can be.

You might need to experiment by combining your elements in different ways to create alternative versions. For example, you may need to alter relative sizes or the position of elements to improve the visual hierarchy or make better use of the space available.

You must get feedback from others at each stage of the process. Make sure you keep a record of this feedback and what you did about it.

Can I do this?

Using artwork and imaging software, make sure you can:

Choose appropriate file formats

Prepare images for print

Prepare images for screen

▸▸ Activity 5.15

Create a prototype of your Cafe 21 home page, using your storyboard to help you. Ask your test users for comments and keep repeating the production cycle until you are happy with the product.

What if you can't build a prototype?

You will be able to produce a home page or a poster, but do you have access to a pottery kiln for your mug? Will the technology department help you to produce a sign for the cafe? Have you got a printer that can produce a full-size net for your kids' pack? There will always be products that you can design but can't actually make yourself. How can you show people what these products would look like?

- **Scale models** can be used to represent larger products. For example, you could produce an accurate scaled version of your kids' pack. The same applies to any printed product.
- **Mock-ups** can be built to represent the real thing. If you make a mock-up of a mug, the surface elements need to be accurately reproduced in the correct colours, and be correctly sized and positioned. You might print the elements on paper or transparent film, cut them out and stick them onto a plain mug.
- **ICT tools** can be used to create digital representations of products. For example, to represent the mug you could use photographs of a mug taken from different angles and add the graphic elements as they would look in the finished product.

You could make a mock-up of a gift bag or create a digital representation

TALKING POINT 5.8

In THE PROJECT *there are some products for which you cannot produce prototypes. What is the best way to represent them?*

▸▸ Activity 5.16

Produce two representations of your mug: a mock-up using any plain mug and a digital representation using ICT tools. Show both to your test users. Which method works best for them? Keep repeating the production cycle until you are happy with the product.

▸▸ Activity 5.17

Use your design to create an accurate representation of your kids' pack. Ask your test users for comments. Did they find your representation helpful? Keep repeating the production cycle until you are happy with the product.

How is DiDA assessed?

Exhibiting your work on screen

Hopefully you will get the chance to exhibit your collection of graphic products to a live audience, show off your kids' pack and even serve tea in your mug. But how can you present your work to people further afield? An eportfolio provides the answer.

Some of your graphic products will be designed to be viewed on screen. For others you will have created digital representations, but what do you do about the print-based prototypes and products like your box and your poster?

You need to find ways of showing the prototypes on screen. You could take photographs from different angles, produce a short movie or a 360° pan of a product or add a voiceover to explain the product. Try to be creative: if it's an item of clothing, get someone to model it, or if it's a poster, display it on a wall.

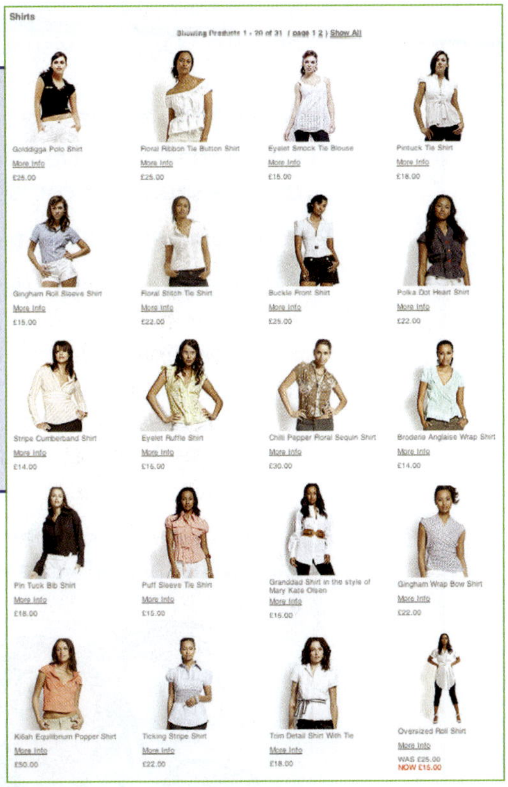

▸▸ Activity 5.18

Explore some websites for clothing, signs and other graphic products to see how products can be shown off to the best advantage. Look at ASOS and Tate Online to start you off.

On eBay, sellers have to promote their own products using photographs – how well do they do it?

Download times

How many times have you got fed up with waiting for images to download on a website? Make sure that you optimise your graphic products and representations so that your audience doesn't lose interest.

TALKING POINT 5.9

What is a reasonable download time? How long do you usually wait for an image to download before giving up and looking elsewhere?

▸▸ Activity 5.19

Decide how you will show off your kids' pack in your eportfolio. How about showing it with food in it? How many shots do you need? Create the images ready for your eportfolio. Check the file sizes.

Tackling THE PROJECT

P

Developing your products

It is now time to complete the production cycle for all the products. You have already made a good start by producing detailed designs, gathering the elements you need and even producing some of the final products and representations. Review your work on the kids' pack, the mug and the home page. Have you fully tested each one? Would you be happy to publish them? If not, what else needs to be done?

Build prototypes or representations for the cafe sign and for the poster. Ask your test users for feedback and make changes. Don't be fooled into thinking that these are the easy ones. This unit is about using graphics to communicate information and this applies to all the products.

Keep repeating the production cycle for all the products until you are satisfied that they are fit for purpose. Look at the complete suite of products. They are all for Cafe 21. Is that obvious? Do your visual links work?

Sorting the evidence

Check that you have safely stored the evidence you need for your eportfolio. All your designs should, of course, be annotated to show feedback and to explain your decisions.

Your evidence is likely to include:

- **logo:** initial design, detailed design and the final logo
- **sign:** initial design, storyboard and a representation of the sign
- **poster:** initial design, detailed design and the final poster
- **mug:** initial design, final design, mock-up and representation
- **home page:** initial design, detailed storyboard and the final page
- **kids' pack:** initial design, final design for the net and representation(s) of the final product.

In each case, make sure that you have prepared the evidence for your eportfolio in ways that will show off your work on screen. Take particular care with the print-based products.

6 Showcasing your achievements

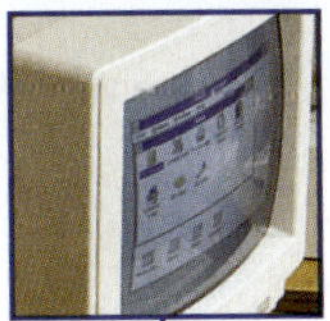

You are now the proud owner of some exciting and original graphic products. Your eportfolio should be a showcase for these and it would be a shame if it does not do them justice.

Take the opportunity to make use of your graphics skills to produce an eportfolio that is a graphic product in its own right.

First impressions are important, so make sure your home page does the trick. A graphical user interface is a must and you can help the user by including graphics on the navigation bar.

Find the best way of exhibiting each product. You will need to be particularly careful with products that are not designed to be viewed on screen.

Don't forget that the production cycle is as important for the eportfolio as it is for the products. Allow plenty of time for design and prototyping and choose your test users with care.

In this chapter you will learn how to exhibit your work in an eportfolio by:

- *organising the content*
- *designing an appropriate structure*
- *using graphics to enhance the user experience*
- *prototyping and testing to ensure fitness for purpose*

Getting started

This is your big chance to display all your hard work. Don't spoil the effect by skimping on the effort you put into designing and creating your eportfolio. Remember that it is a graphic product in its own right. There are some important decisions to make. You need to decide on the:

- evidence you want to include
- structure and navigation
- content and layout of each page
- colour scheme
- graphic elements, including navigational aids
- presentation styles.

Don't forget everything you have learned about the design process. Get some feedback on initial and detailed designs before you start to build the eportfolio.

You should already have thought about how to show off your work at its best, especially products that are not designed for on screen publication. Check that your representations do the job.

Getting organised

First you should check that you have produced everything that is required for your eportfolio. Do you have everything listed in the project brief? Make sure that you include evidence of how you progressed from initial ideas, through designs, to the final products.

Adding content to your eportfolio is like packing a suitcase for a holiday: put in too much and you will run into trouble because you have excess baggage! The golden rule of packing is to leave out anything you will not actually use on your holiday. Use this rule with your eportfolio and make sure that everything you add has a specific purpose.

Don't forget that you must use only file formats listed in the brief. Check all your files and convert them if necessary.

Activity 6.1

Look at all the work you have produced for The Project. Sort your files into three categories:

- **essential content, including everything on the checklist**
- **useful supporting evidence**
- **excess baggage – leave it out!**

Are all the files in acceptable formats? Convert any that are not and remove the original versions.

Acknowledging sources

Make sure that your elements table is complete and you have information about every element including:

- file name (including extension, for example cyclist.jpg)
- description of the element
- whether it came from a primary or secondary source
- full details of the source
- how you have adapted it
- where it was used
- details of permissions.

Don't forget to include elements from both primary and secondary sources. You can only gain credit for the elements you have created yourself if you make it clear what they are and where to find them.

▸▸ Activity 6.2

Make sure that you have fully acknowledged all the sources in your eportfolio for THE PROJECT, both primary and secondary.

Making navigation easy

Users don't want to get lost looking for evidence. Use a structure chart to ensure that you create a logical structure and make it easy for them to find their way around.

▸▸ Activity 6.3

Create a structure chart for THE PROJECT eportfolio showing how the pages will link together.

How will the user move around your eportfolio? On every page of your eportfolio you will need to include links to products and supporting information. Text links are one option, but why not use graphic elements to provide a visual link to each item? For example, you could use a thumbnail image of each product in a navigation bar.

For consistency, you should place navigational aids in the same position on every page.

▸▸ Activity 6.4

Design graphical navigation aids for your eportfolio for THE PROJECT.

Designing the pages

From the outset you should be thinking about the look and feel you want to achieve and what types of graphic element you want to use on the pages of your eportfolio. Use a storyboard to design the content and layout of the pages.

Don't forget to think about visual hierarchy on each page. What do you want to draw attention to first?

Home page

Your home page is your 'shop window'. How can you persuade people that it is going to be a good experience to go inside and look around? You must include specified details about yourself, but that alone won't make a very exciting home page for the user.

TALKING POINT 6.1

How can graphics be used on the home page to enhance the user's experience? What might annoy or distract them?

Summary of contents

Your home page needs some sort of introduction to the eportfolio, what it's about and what is in it.

Use graphic elements to illustrate the text. For example, your eportfolio for The Project might include a collage of elements used in your products or a stylised portrait of yourself.

How effective is this student's home page?

Context pages

Use your context pages to set the scene for each piece of evidence so that the user gets a really good idea of what you are presenting and how you achieved it. This is a good place to explain some of your design decisions. Use graphic elements to illustrate what you have to say.

▸▸ Activity 6.5

Produce a storyboard for each page of your eportfolio. Use the structure chart you created earlier to help you. It should show:

- **what will appear on each page**
- **the position of the elements on the pages**
- **the colours, fonts and font sizes you will use.**

▸▸ Activity 6.6

Build your eportfolio using your storyboards and structure chart to help you.

Does it do the job?

Making sure the links work

Make sure you do not use the wrong types of links! Remind yourself of the difference between relative and absolute links. The rules are quite simple:

- **Relative links** are used to link to other files within your eportfolio.
- **Absolute links** are used *only* when you want to link to something outside the eportfolio, such as a website.

▸▸ Activity 6.7

Make sure that all links to files within the eportfolio are relative, not absolute. If you can, check it on a stand-alone machine to make sure that all the links work.

Accessibility

You should include accessibility features in your eportfolio to make sure that users have no trouble finding and viewing all the content.

▸▸ Activity 6.8

Add accessibility features such as alt-text and resizable fonts if you haven't done so already. Ask others to comment on these features.

Does it have the 'feel good factor'?

Have you made effective use of graphics tools to showcase your achievements and enhance the user experience?

- Is your eportfolio eye-catching and original?
- Have you used graphics to good effect throughout the eportfolio, not just in the final products?
- Is the navigation clear and consistent?
  - Are links and buttons are easy to spot?
  - Do the graphics make it clear where the links go?
- Is the layout clear and consistent?
  - Is the navigation bar in the same place on every page?
  - Are the pages well laid out and uncluttered?
- Are colour schemes consistent and effective?
- Do all the graphics load quickly enough?
- Are all the graphics positioned correctly and do they all appear?
- Is the eportfolio as accessible as possible?
  - Are accessibility features clear to the user?

Does this eportfolio have the 'feel good factor'?

Repeat the testing process until you can answer 'Yes' to each of these questions.

▸▸ Activity 6.9

Make sure that your eportfolio has the 'feel good factor'!

Project review

Did you get everything right first time? What can you learn from your experiences? You should carry out an end-of-project review that looks at:

- your graphic products
- the project as a whole
- your own performance.

Don't just give a step-by-step description of everything you did. The important thing is to make judgements about each aspect. Think about improvements you would make if you had more time and how you will do things differently in future.

Other people's opinions matter here. Ask them to comment on each aspect. It's too late to change what you have done, but you can learn from the feedback and use it to help you write your review. Don't feel you have to agree with everything they say. If you disagree, explain why.

TALKING POINT 6.2

How will you cope when a reviewer spots a mistake in your work that you can't change?

Reviewing your own performance

Reviewing your own performance is probably the hardest part of the review process, but it is something you will get better at with practice. You need to be really honest with yourself. The idea is to learn from your experiences.

TALKING POINT 6.3

How can graphic elements be used to enhance your project review?

▸▸ Activity 6.10

Review your work on THE PROJECT. Use your graphics skills to present your review in a creative way. Add your review to your eportfolio and make sure that the links work.

And finally…

What else is left to do?

Test, test and test again!

You and your test users need to check that:

- the content is correct, containing
  - all the evidence and nothing unnecessary
  - the final version in each case, not an earlier one by mistake
- the content works as intended
  - all products and supporting evidence display clearly on screen
  - each product works as intended when run from within the eportfolio
- the links and hyperlinks work as intended
  - all links go where they should
  - every item of content has a link to it
- accessibility features work
  - alternative text
  - resizable fonts
- the product works in a range of different browsers
- the complete eportfolio meets the technical specification, including file formats and overall size.

TALKING POINT 6.4

Take each of these checks in turn and discuss what you need to do to test your eportfolio properly.

Who else should test your eportfolio?

Test your eportfolio yourself first then ask others to test if for you, preferably on a computer that is not linked to your network or the internet. This should show any incorrect links or missing images.

You should consider the feedback you are given and decide if you need to make any changes. Record the feedback and any action you take in your review.

You can collect feedback from a wide range of different people, including your peers, teachers and other adults. When you do the real SPB, remember that the audience is the moderator – so choose your test users carefully.

Activity 6.11

Test your eportfolio for THE PROJECT to make sure that it works both on your computer and on a standalone machine. Work in groups and test the final eportfolios for each other.

Skills list

Bitmap-based software tools

Internet and intranets

- Refresh the browser
- Navigate through pages
- Use page history
- Bookmark a page
- Use hyperlinks within sites
- Copy and save information
- Print a page
- Use one criterion in a search engine
- Use multiple criteria in a search engine
- Refine a search in a search engine

Presentation software

- Create and use colour schemes
- Import and position images
- Format text
- Align images
- Crop and resize images
- Colour images

Word processing software

- Enter and amend text
- Align a paragraph
- Use bullets and numbering
- Use tabs
- Indent a paragraph
- Change font
- Change text style
- Change text colour

Index

Edexcel
190 High Holborn
London WC1V 7BH

ISBN-10: 1-84690-117-0
ISBN-13: 978-1-84690-117-1

Designed by Ken Vail Graphic Design
Picture research by Ann Thomson
Index by Indexing Specialists (UK) Ltd

The publisher's policy is to use paper manufactured from sustainable forests.

Acknowledgements

We are grateful to the following for permission to reproduce copyright photographs:

A1pix: pg 31(br), pg 31(ml), pg 56(tml); **The Advertising Archives:** pg 37(tr), pg 51(b), pg 52(ml), pg 52(mr), pg 54(bl), pg 54(br), pg 66(t); **Alamy:** pg 1(tr), pg1(tl), pg1(bl) (Ulana Switucha), pg 1(br), pg 1(ml), pg 11(ml) (James Cheadle), pg 2(tmr) (Atomer Sykes), pg 2(tr) (Richard Levine), pg 2(tml) (View Pictures Ltd), pg 3(tl) (Foodfolio), pg 4(tmr) (David Pearson), pg 10(tl) (Robert Harding Picture Library Ltd), pg 10(mr), pg 11(m) (Alan King), pg 10(ml) (Jack Sullivan), pg 10(br) (Salient Images), pg 10(bm) (Ashley Cooper), pg 11(tl), pg 25(tl) (Blickwinkel), pg 11(tr) (D. Hurst), pg 13(tr), pg 13 (ml), pg 13(bl), pg 56(tr) (The Flight Collection), pg 25(mr) (Howard Harrison), pg 37(ml) (Index Stock), pg 44(tr) (Matthew Ashton), pg 49(br), pg 49(ml) (Photolibrary Wales), pg 54(ml) (Duncan Hale-Sutton), pg 56(tl) (Nick Higham), pg 65(tl) (Peter Titmuss), pg 77(tr) (GOODSHOOT), pg 78 (Colin Hawkins); **CartoonStock.com:** pg 65(b); **Corbis:** pg 2(bl) (Frank May/epa), pg 7(tr) (©2005 Marvel), pg 9(b), pg 68(b) (Royalty-Free), pg 11(mr) (Duomo), pg 53(b) (Lester Lefkowitz), pg 58(tl) (Richard T. Nowitz), pg 58(tm), pg 58(tr) (Bernard Annebicque/Sygma), pg 64(m) (Abedin Taherkenareh); **Dorling Kindersley:** pg 25(tr) (WWF); **Eddie Stobart:** pg 56(tmr); **Getty Images:** pg 2(ltr), pg 31(tr), pg 31(tl), pg 31(bl) (Andreas Rentz), pg 10(bl) (Graeme Robertson), pg 49(tr), pg 49(tl), pg 49(bl) (Ezra Shaw), pg 51(t) (Nigel Merret), pg 61 (Dennis Hallinan), pg 63(tr), pg 63(tl), pg 63(bl) (AFP), pg 63(br), pg 63(ml) (Yoshikazu Tsuno), pg 64(tr) (Justin Sullivan), pg 73(t) (Lisa M. Robinson), pg 77(b), pg 77(l) (VCL/S. Powell); pg 82 (STRDEL); Heinz: pg 10(tm); **©Pearson Longman:** pg 50(t), 58(b); **Photolibrary.com:** pg 11(tm); **Punchstock:** pg 13(br), pg 13(tl), pg 26 (Bob Peterson); **Redferns Music Picture Library:** pg 56(b); **Rex Features:** pg 10(tm), pg 10(tr), pg 65(tr); **Robert Harding Picture Library:** pg 60 (BananaStock); **Superstock:** pg 3(bl) (Ingram publishing), pg 25(ml) (age fotostock), pg 52(tl), pg 52(tml) (Pixtal), pg 52(tm) Superstock,Inc), pg 52 (tr) (Mark Udry), pg 52(tmr) (Den Reader); **Tesco:** pg 56(tm); **Walls:** pg 11(br).

Cover photograph: **GettyImages:** (Alan Powdrill)

Thank you to the following for supplying photographs: **John Tilley**, **Mari Tudor-Jones**

We wish to thank the following sources for the use of their website information and other copyright material:

Able Minds Inc (CyberKids); Amazon.com; ASOS; BBC / CBBC; Blossom Swap; Department for Transport (Think Road Safety); Google™ of Google Inc; Hobbico / Duratrax; Jamba Juice; Ladybird; Lego; National Museum of Scotland; Paper Airplanes (Alex Schultz); Pret a Manger; Puffin; The Radio Times; Snowdon Railway; Tomato Growers' Association / thetomatozone.co.uk; Transport for London; Unilever (Marmite); Virgin Megastores; Virgin Mobile; The Charlie Waller Memorial Trust (studentdepression.org).

Every effort has been made to trace and acknowledge ownership of copyright and we apologise in advance for any unintentional omissions. If any have been overlooked we would be pleased to insert the appropriate acknowledgement at the earliest opportunity.